Color Me

FIERCE

BY: JODIE BEAU

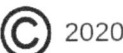 2020

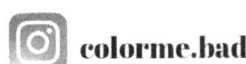 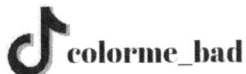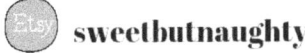

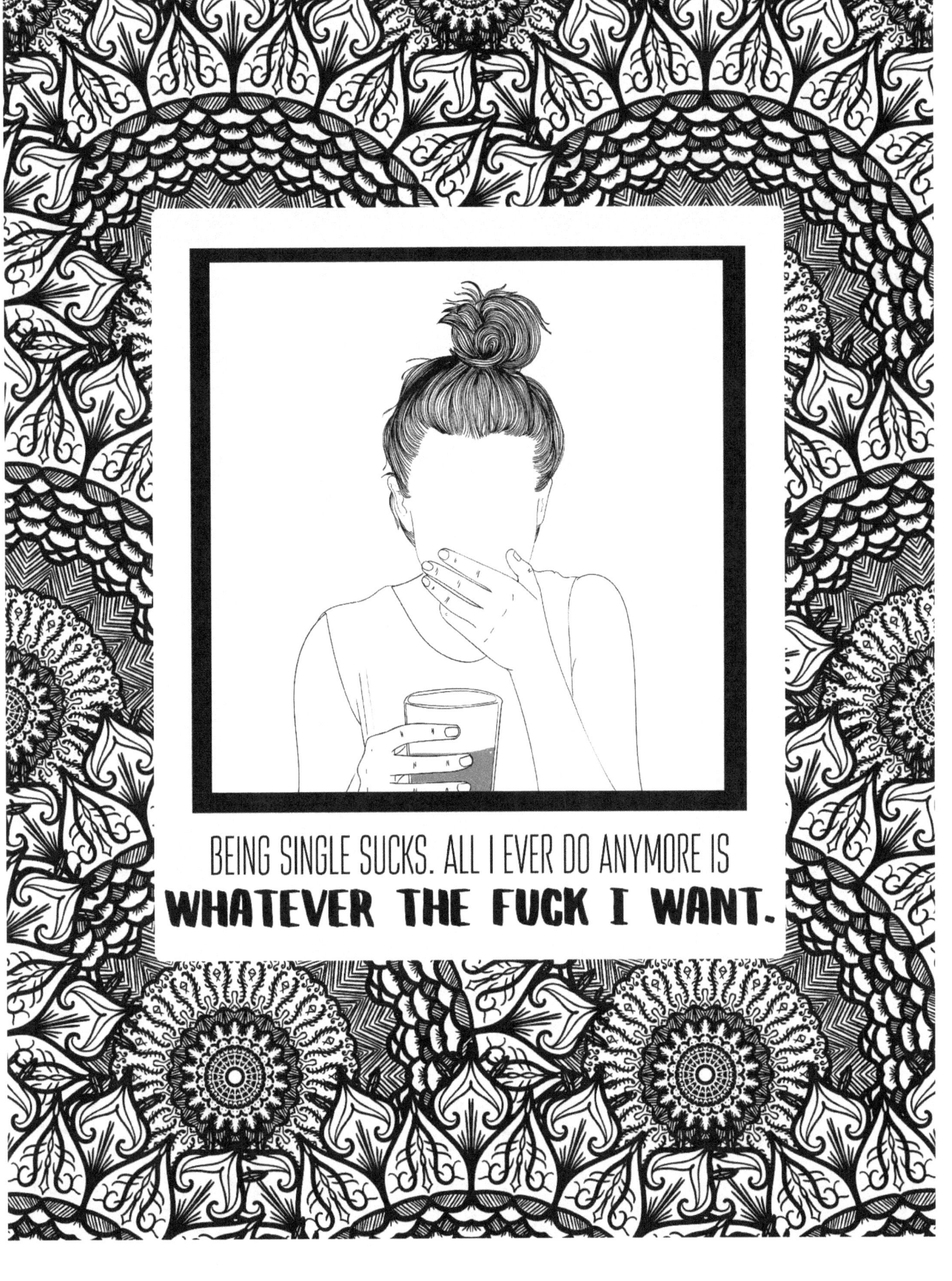

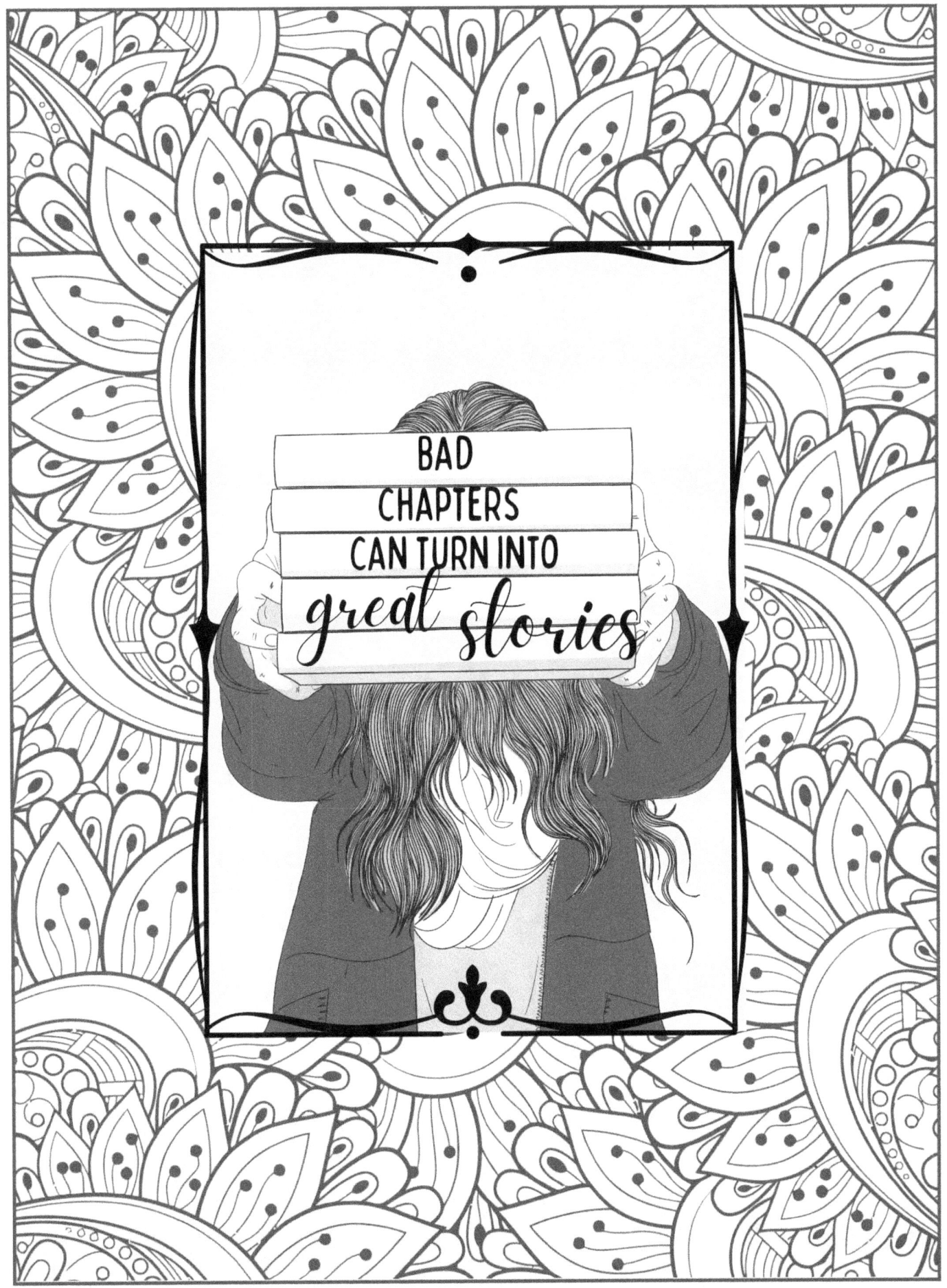

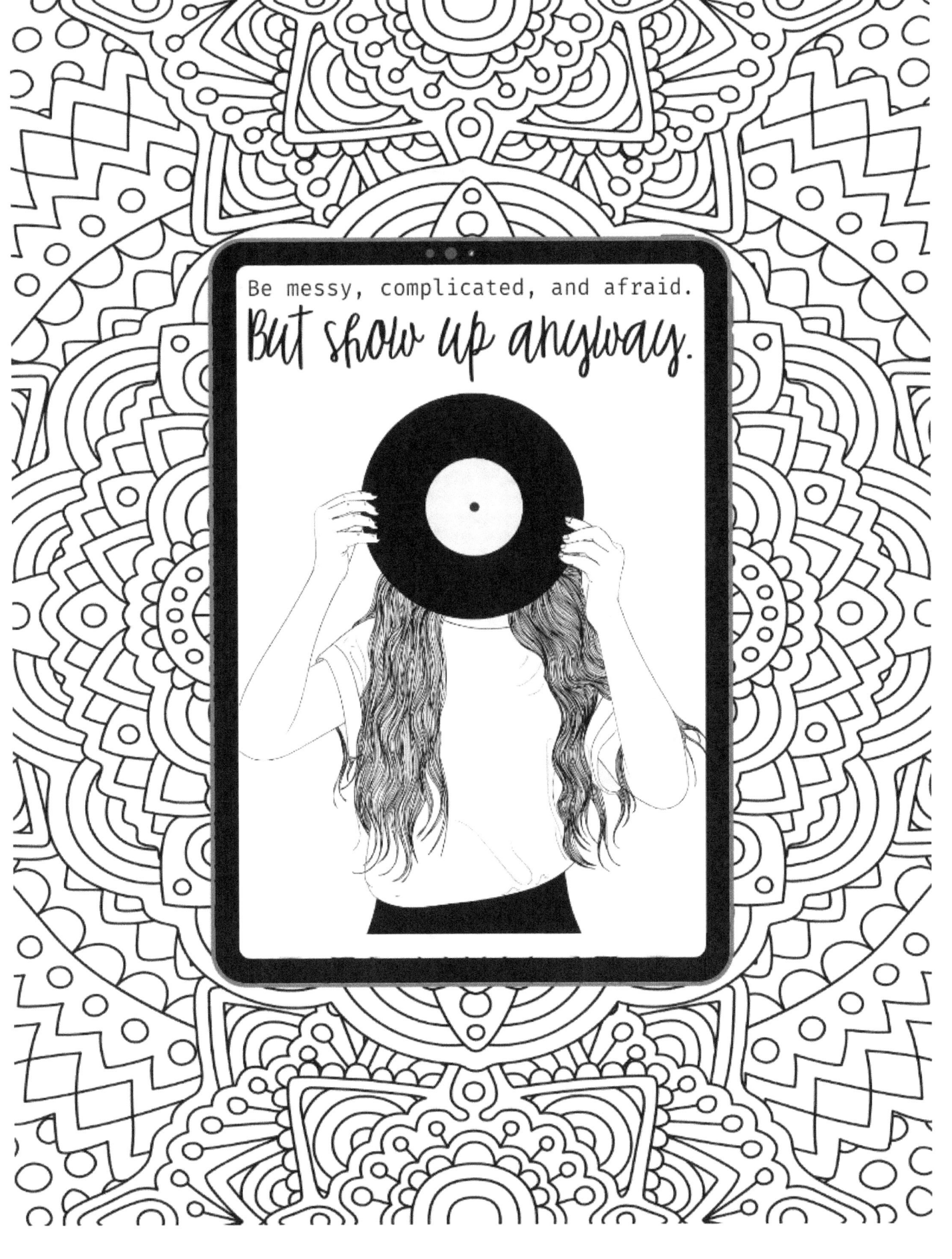

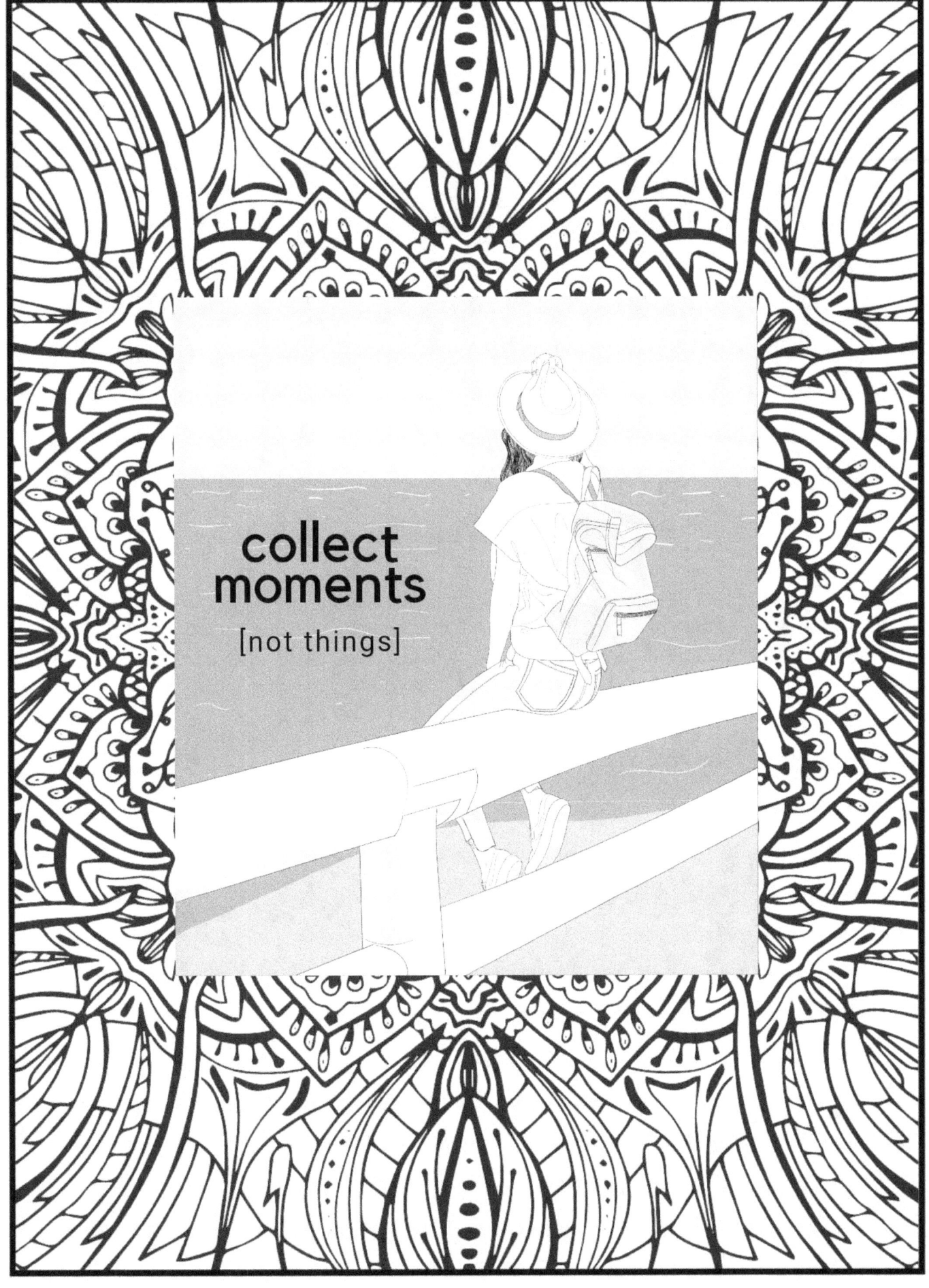

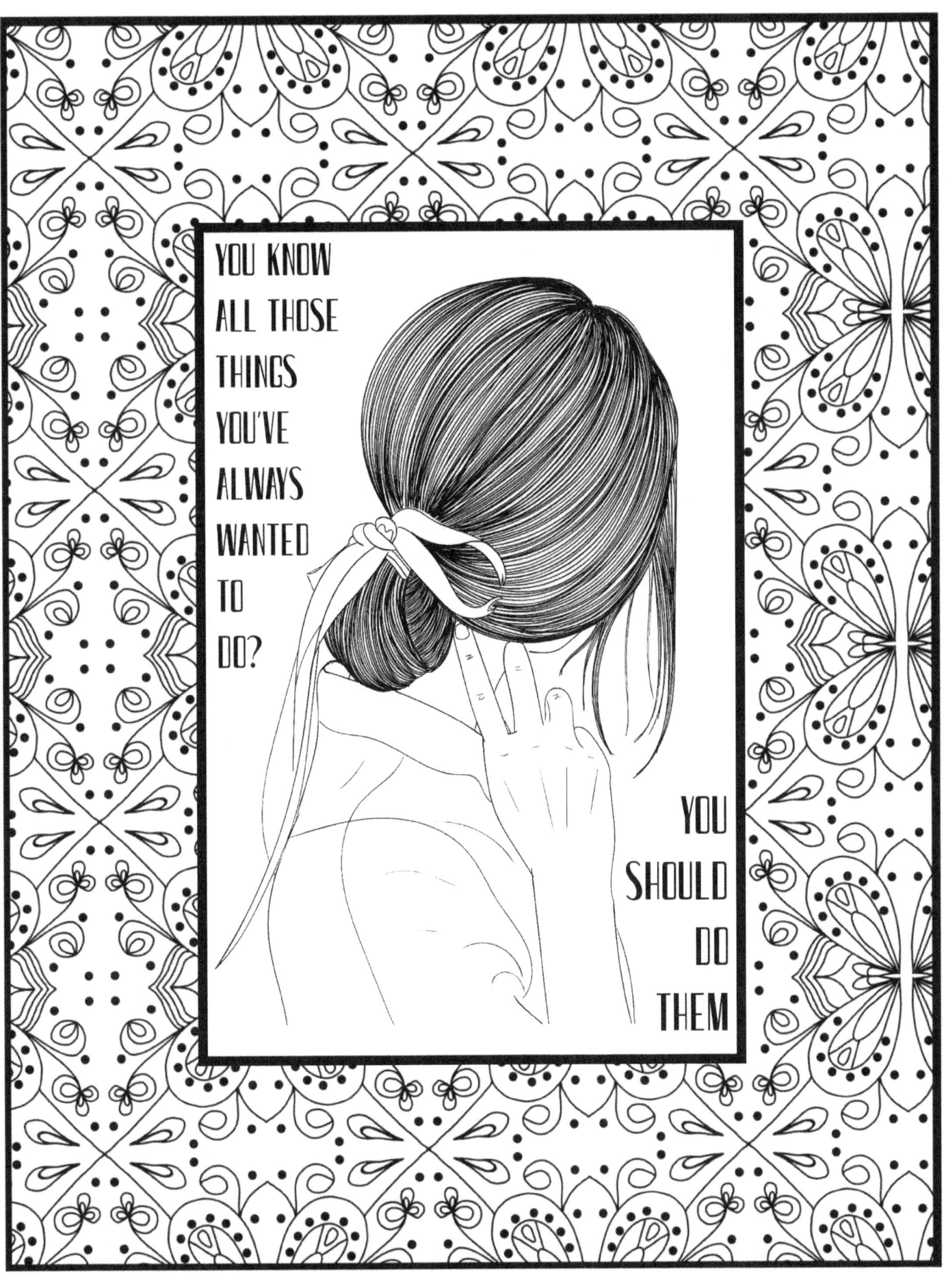

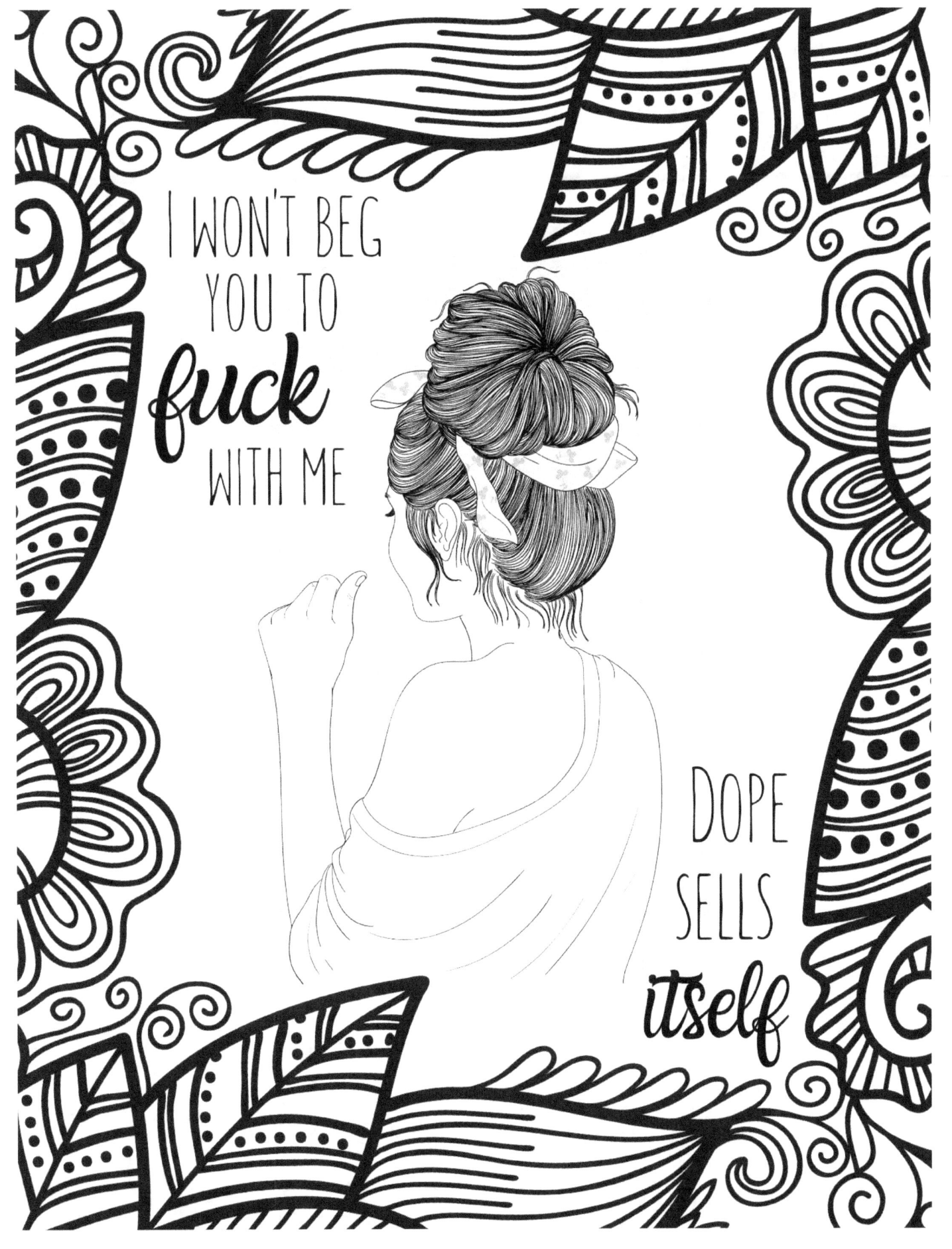

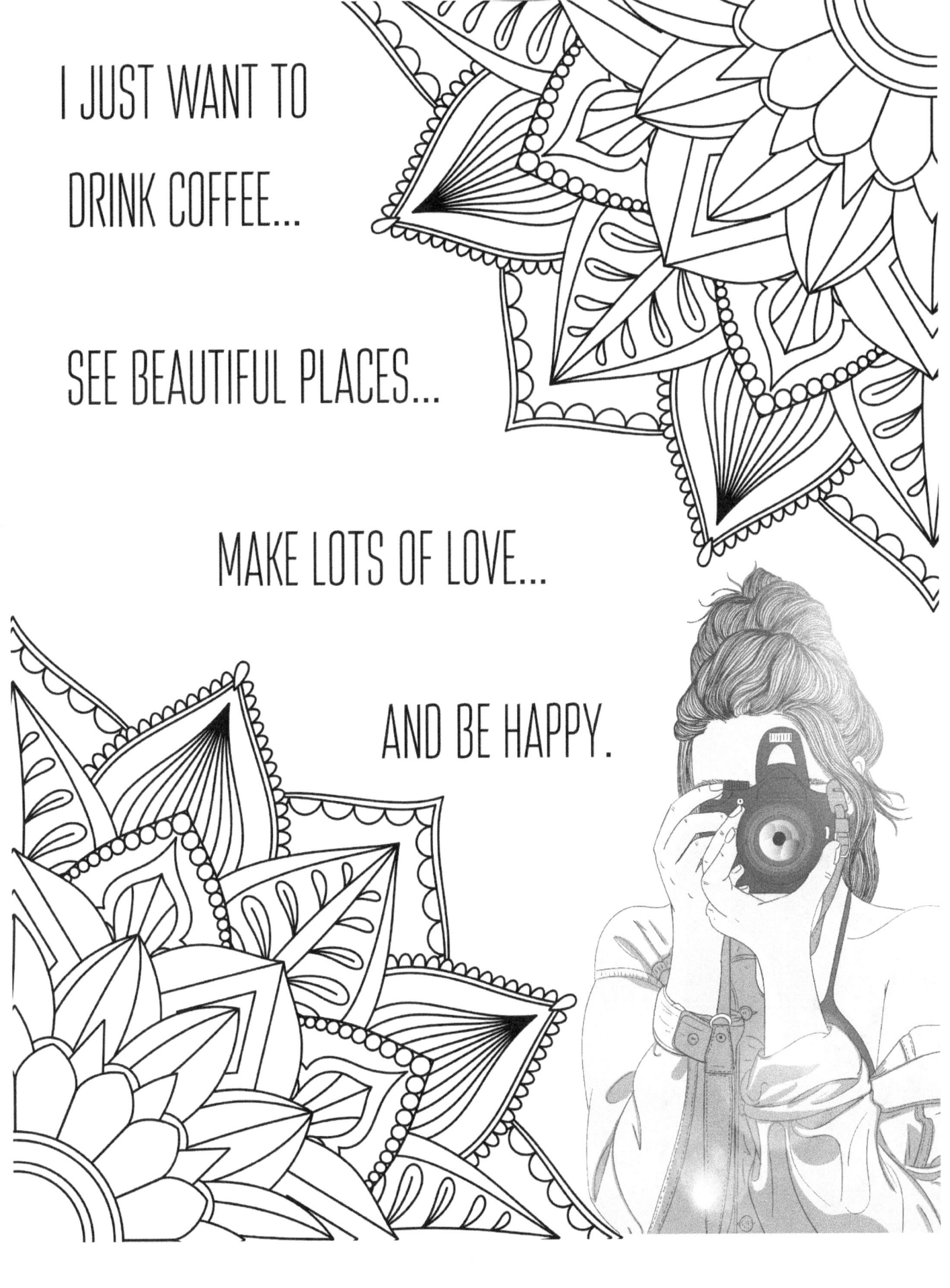

I JUST WANT TO

DRINK COFFEE...

SEE BEAUTIFUL PLACES...

MAKE LOTS OF LOVE...

AND BE HAPPY.

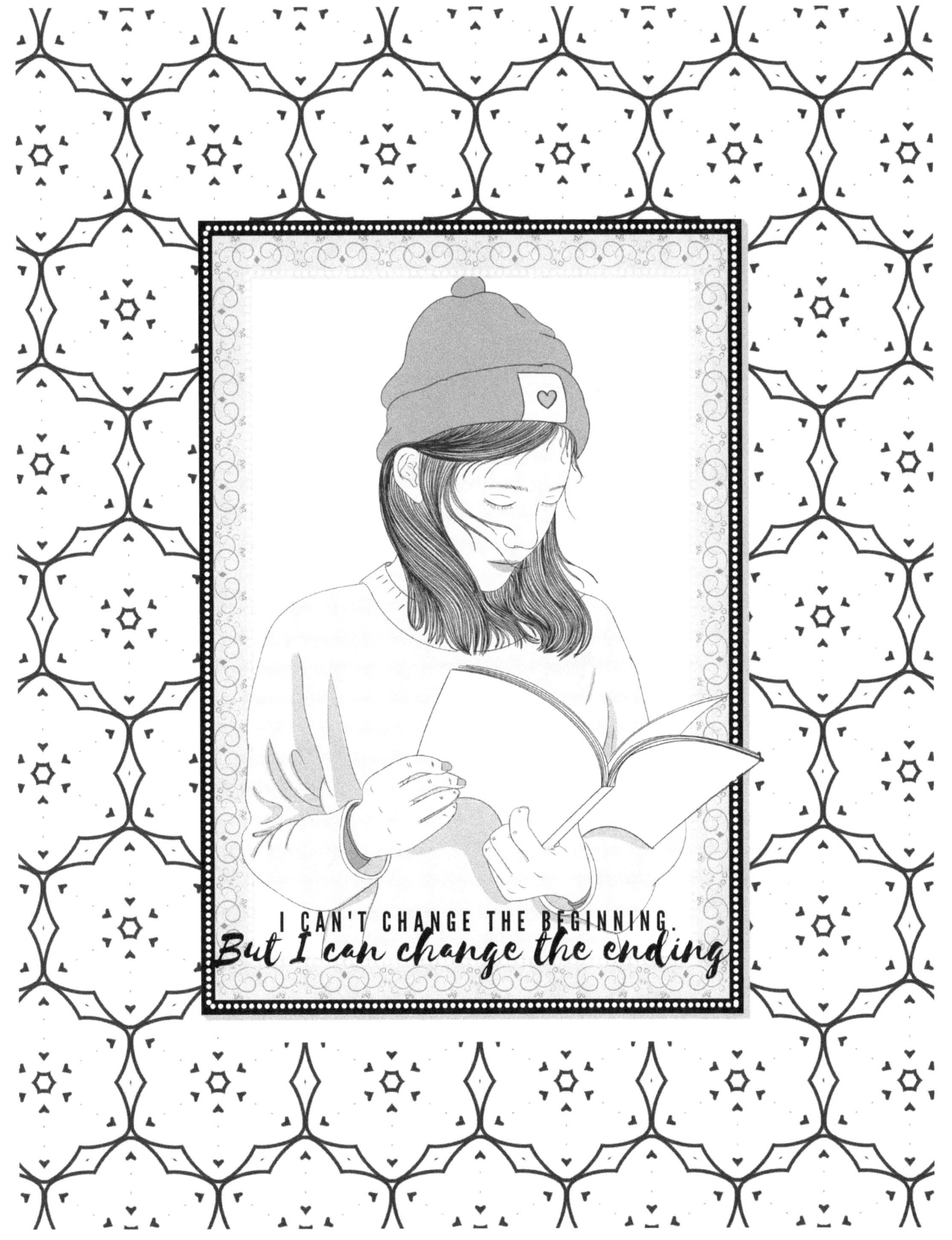

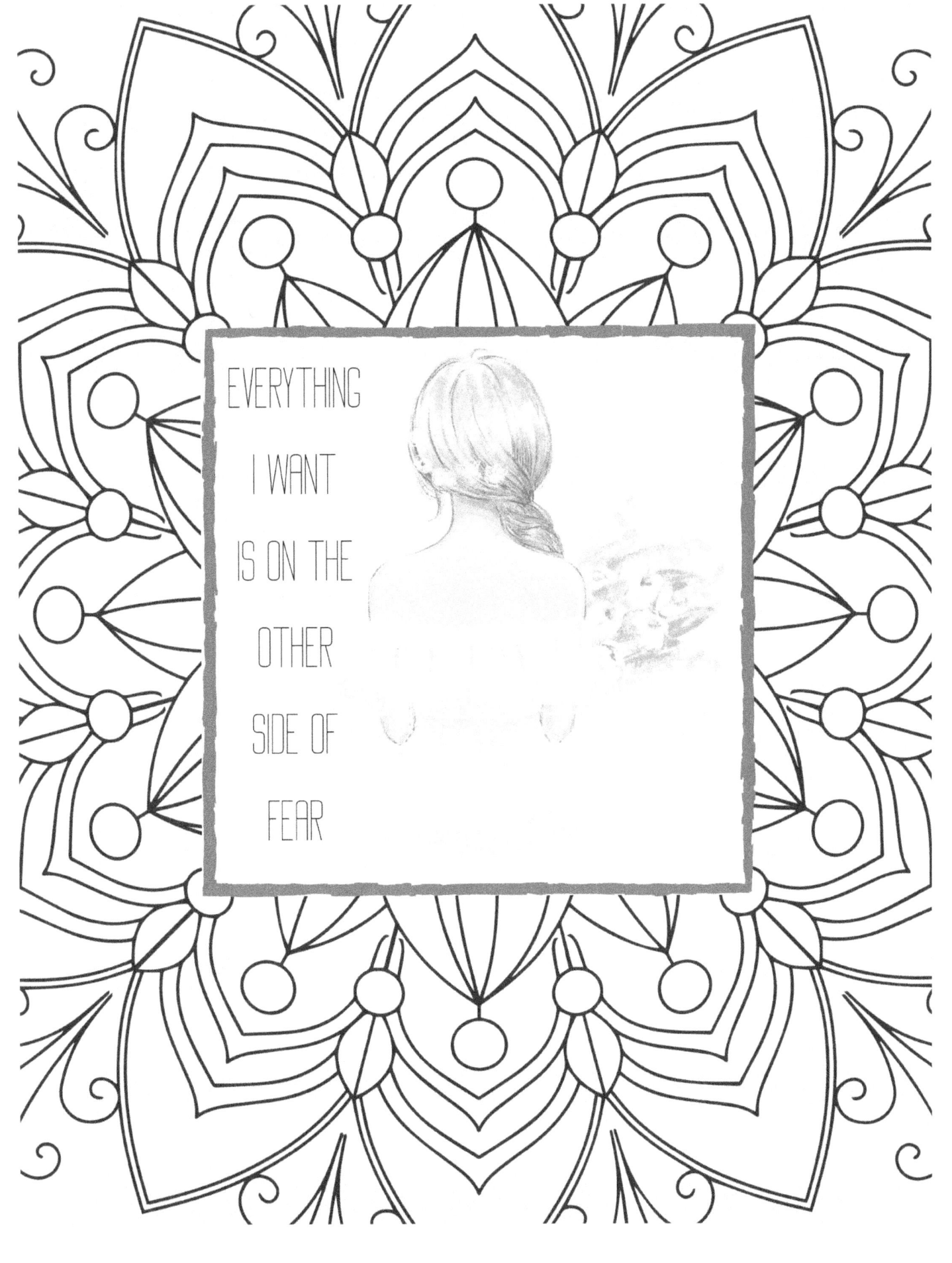

EVERYTHING I WANT IS ON THE OTHER SIDE OF FEAR

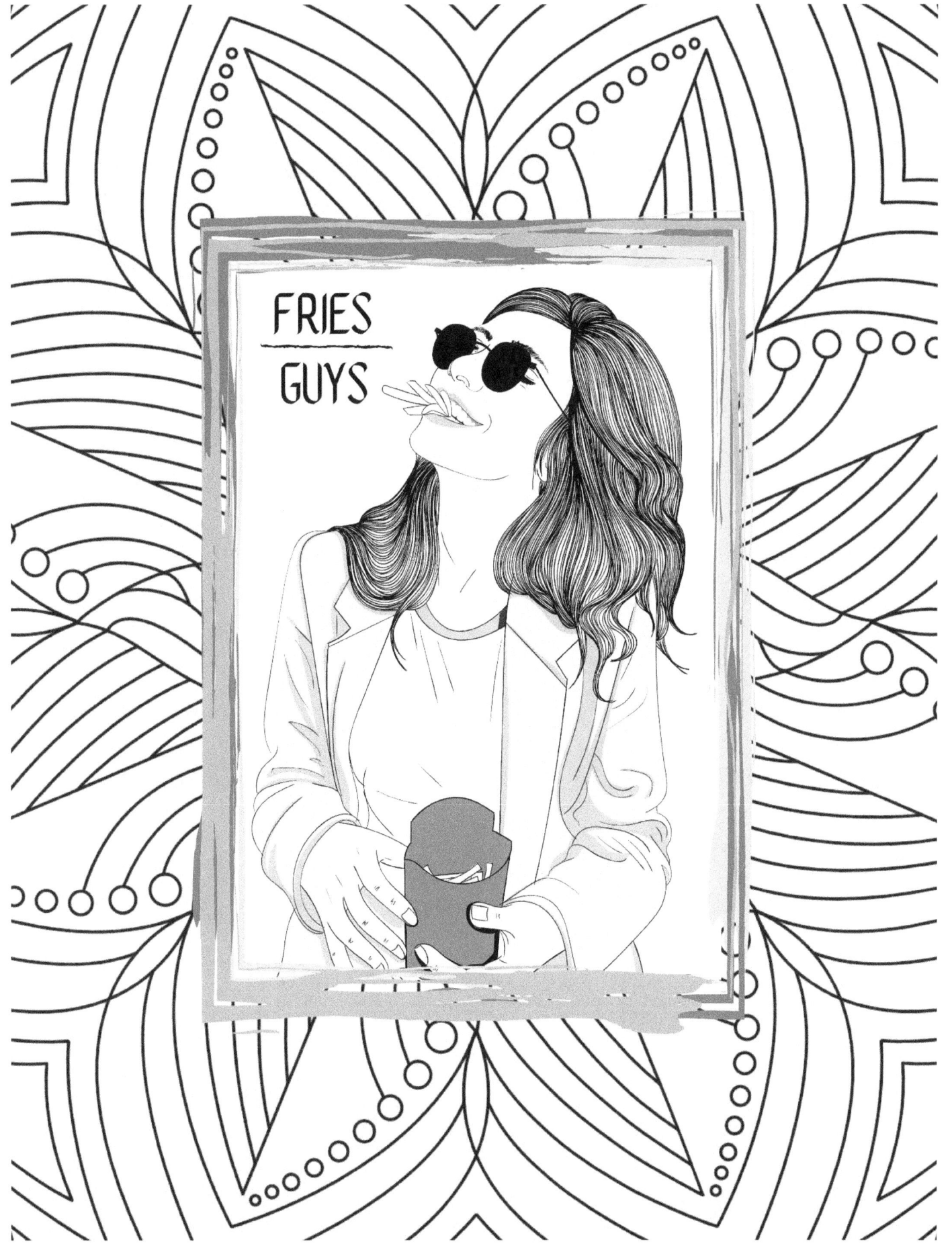

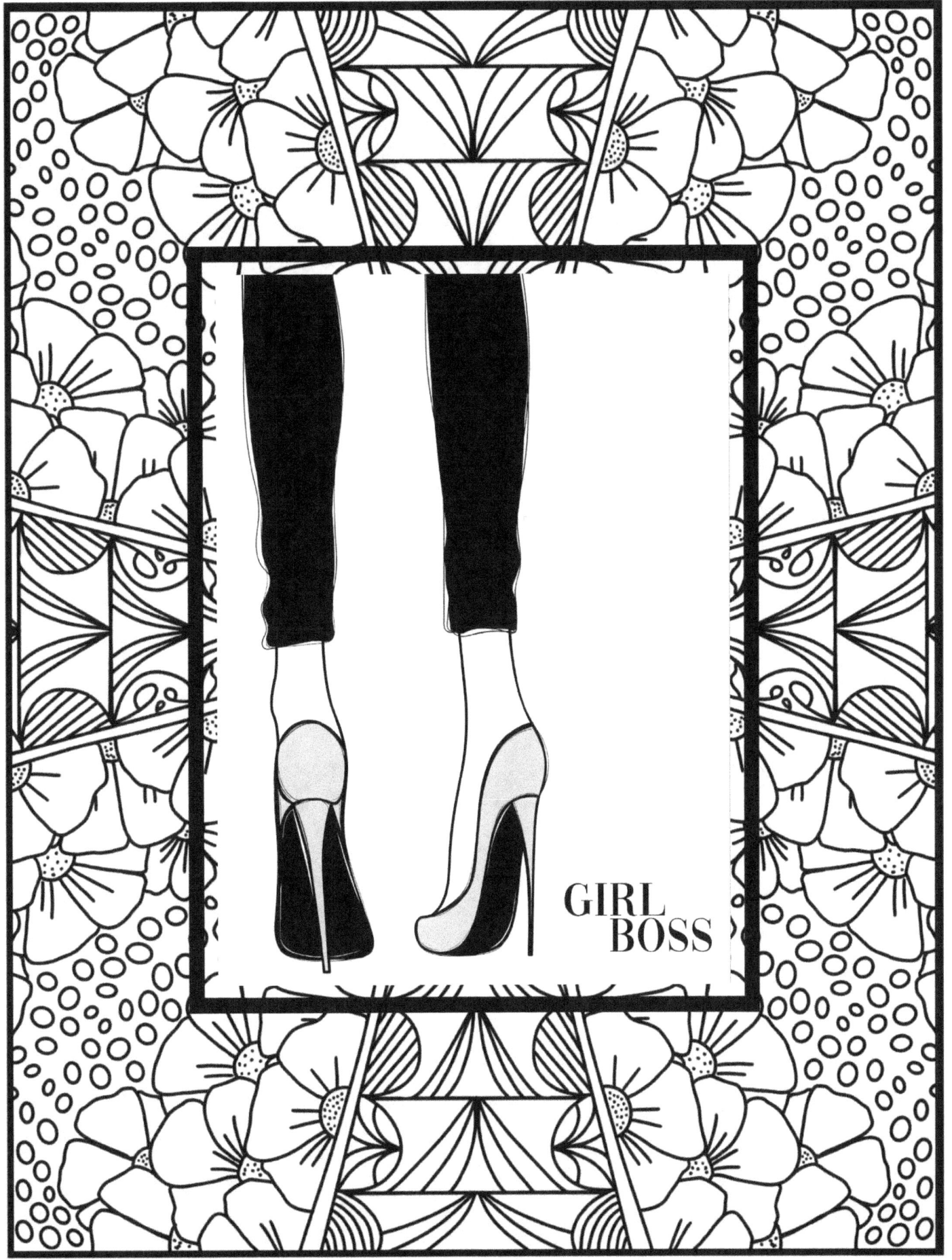

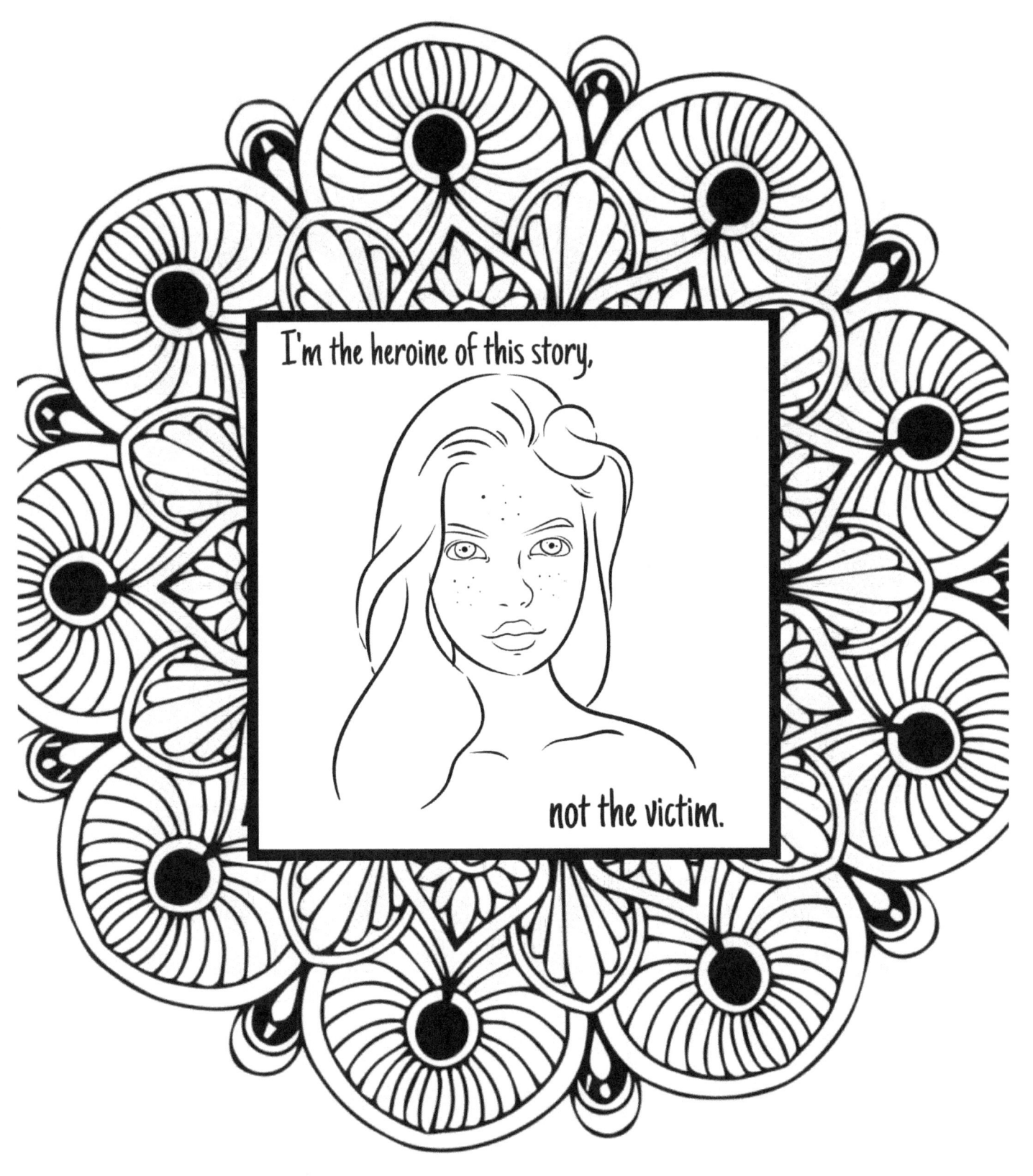

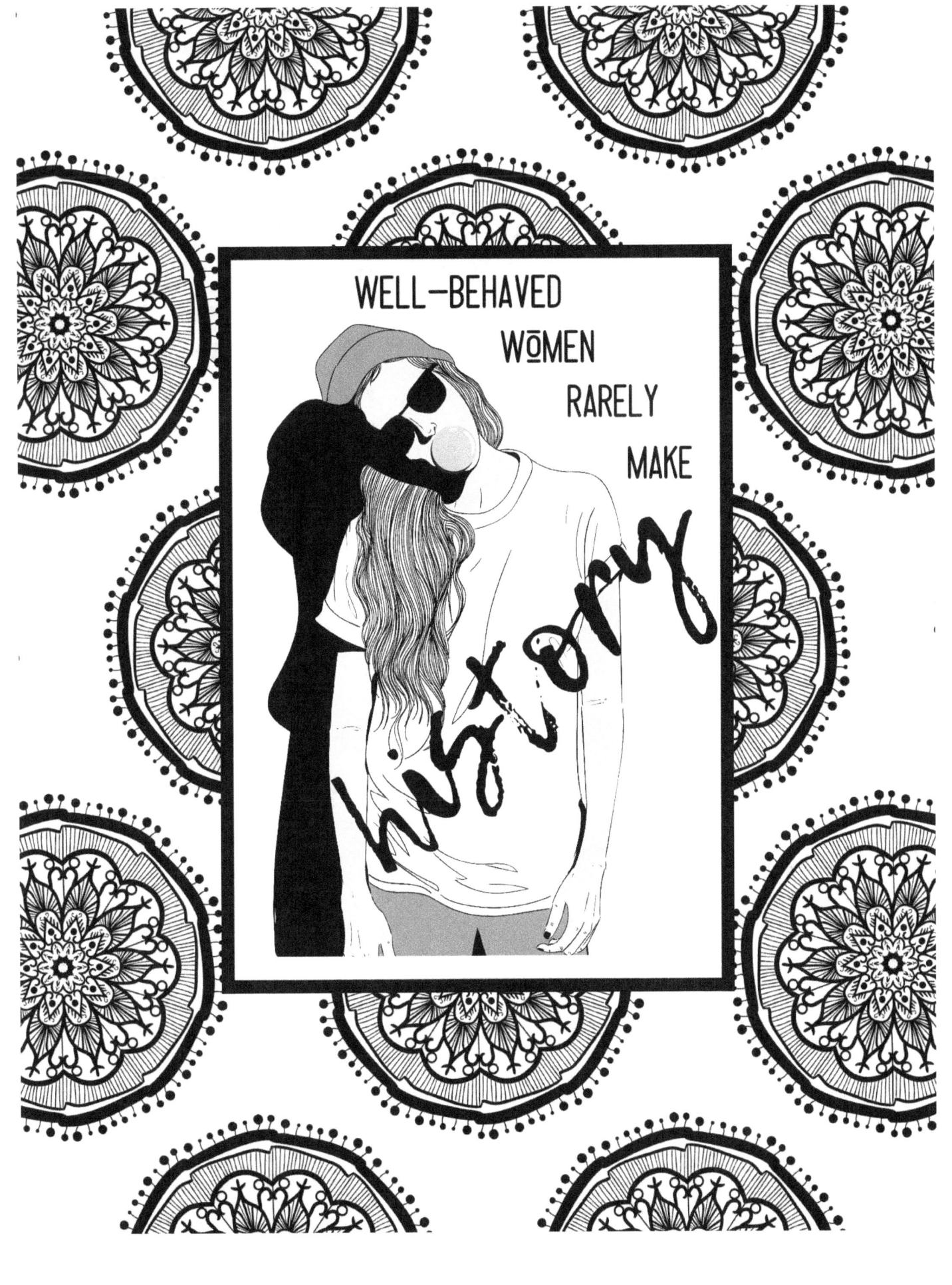

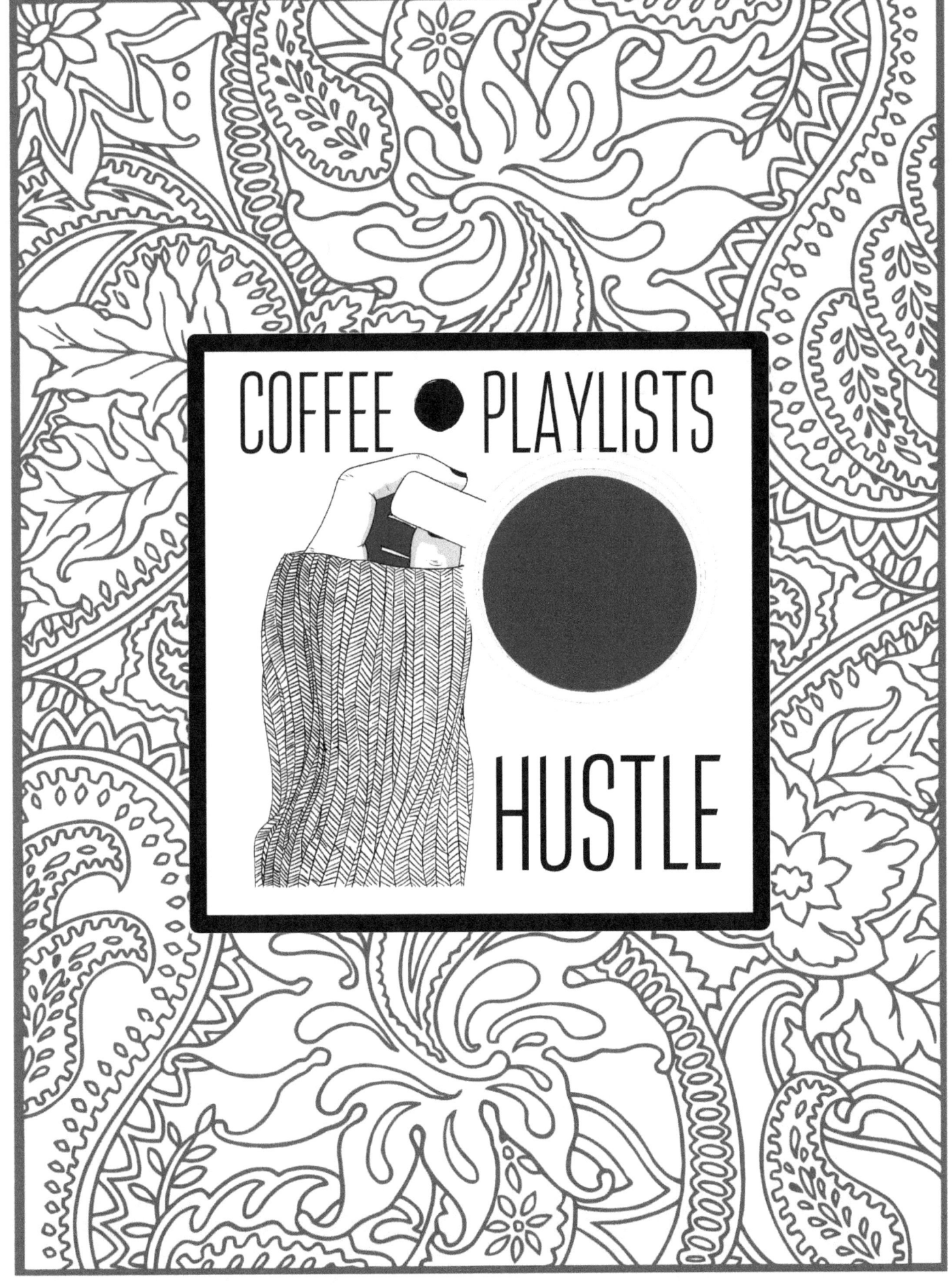

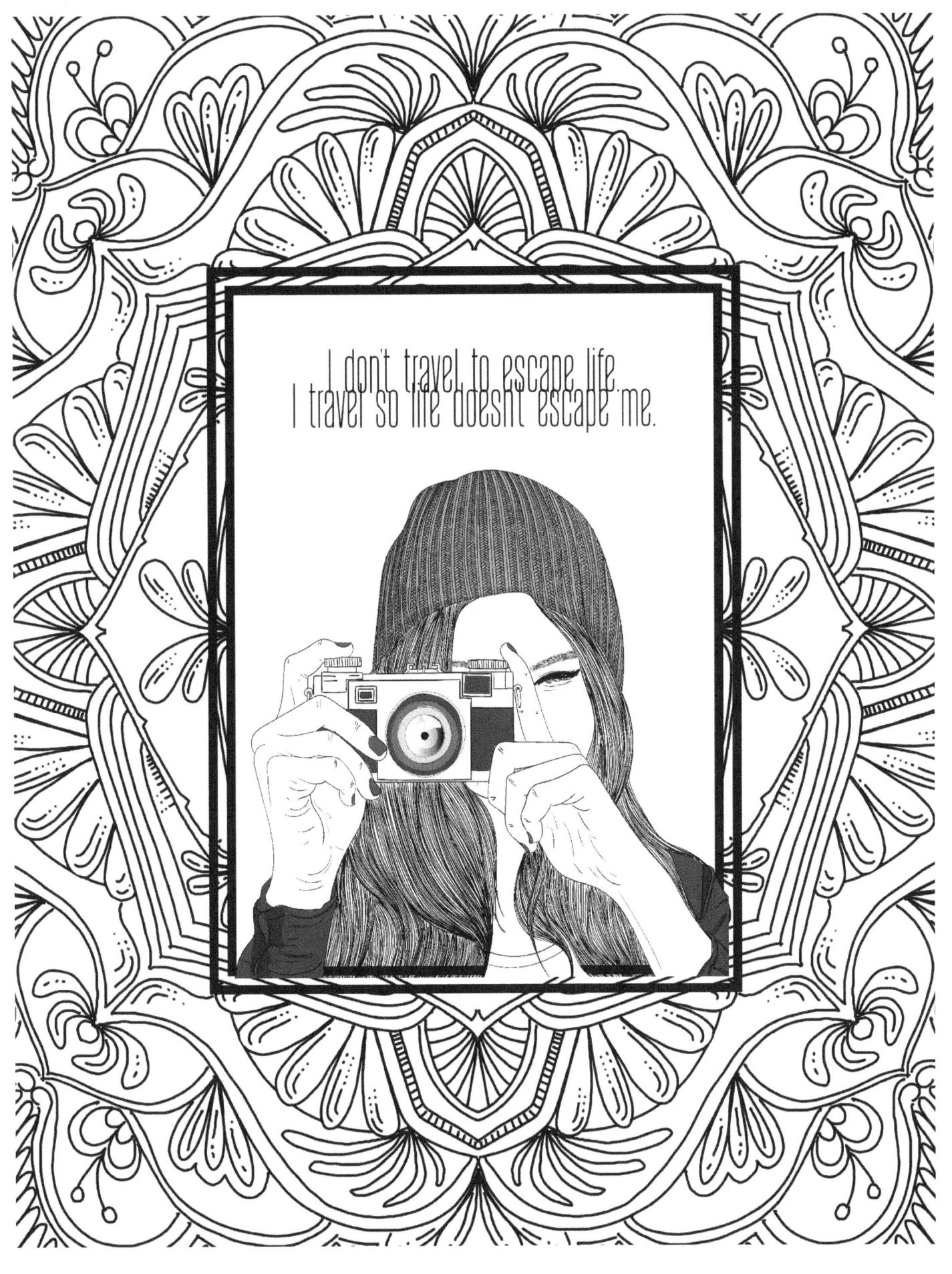

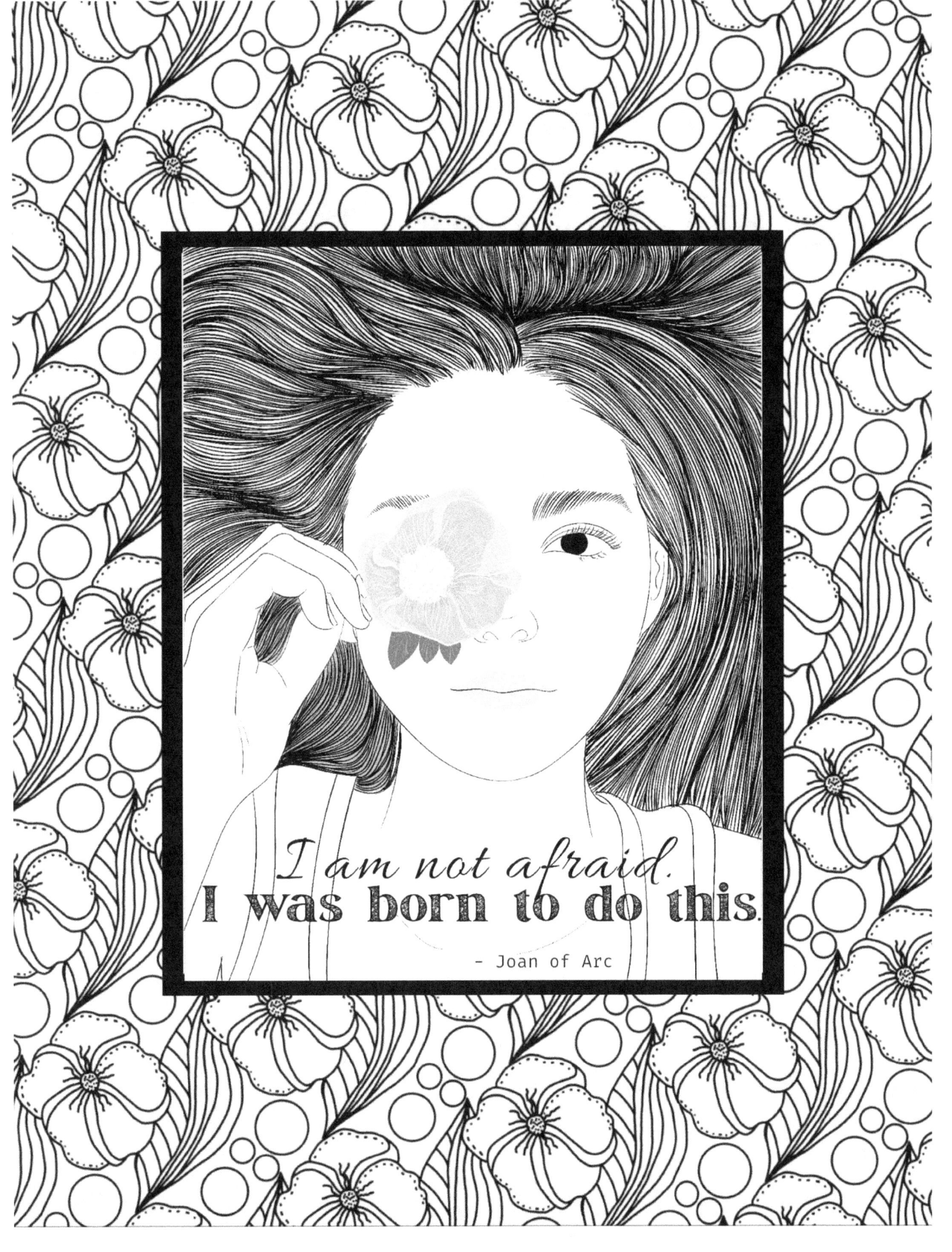

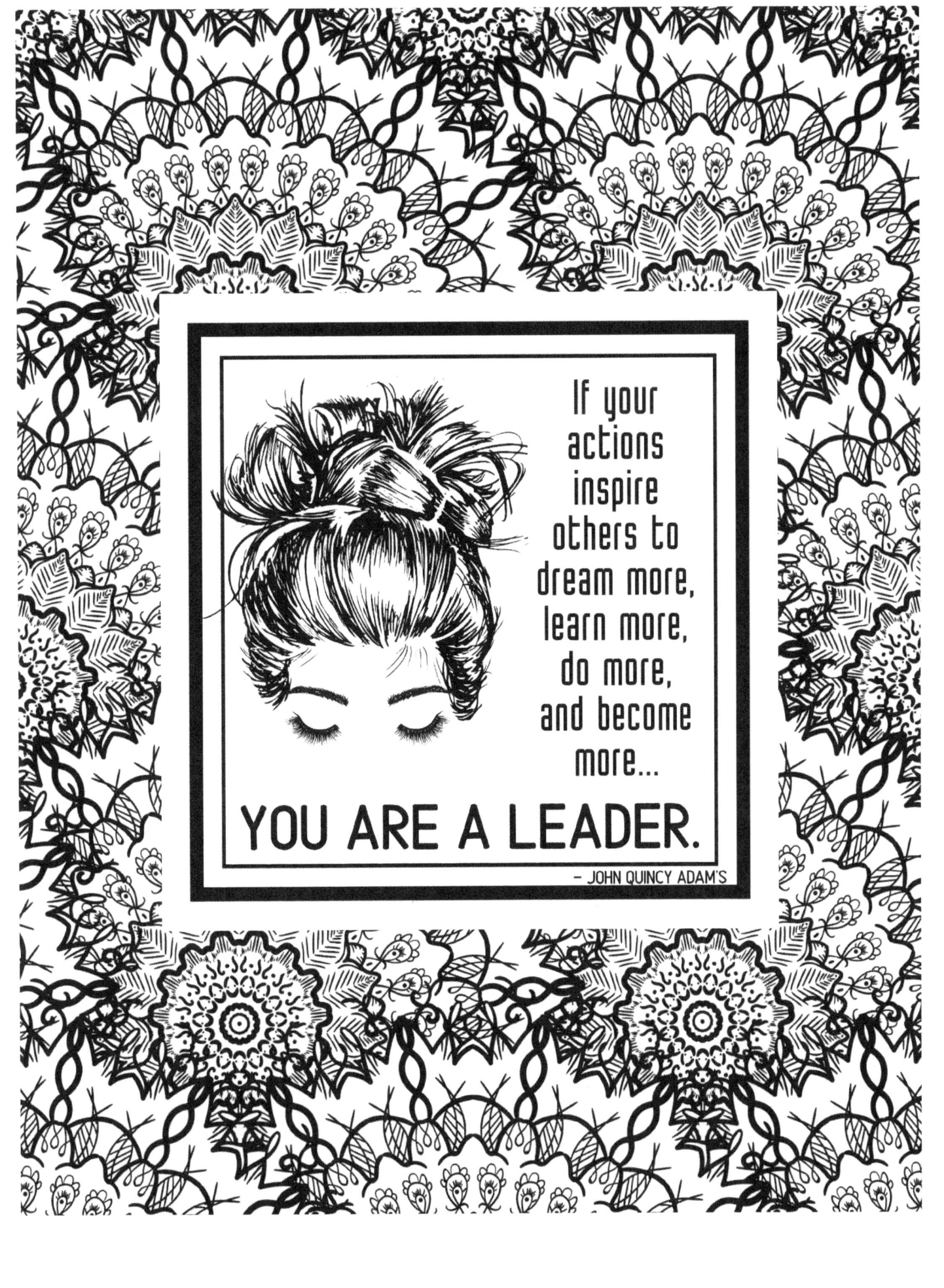

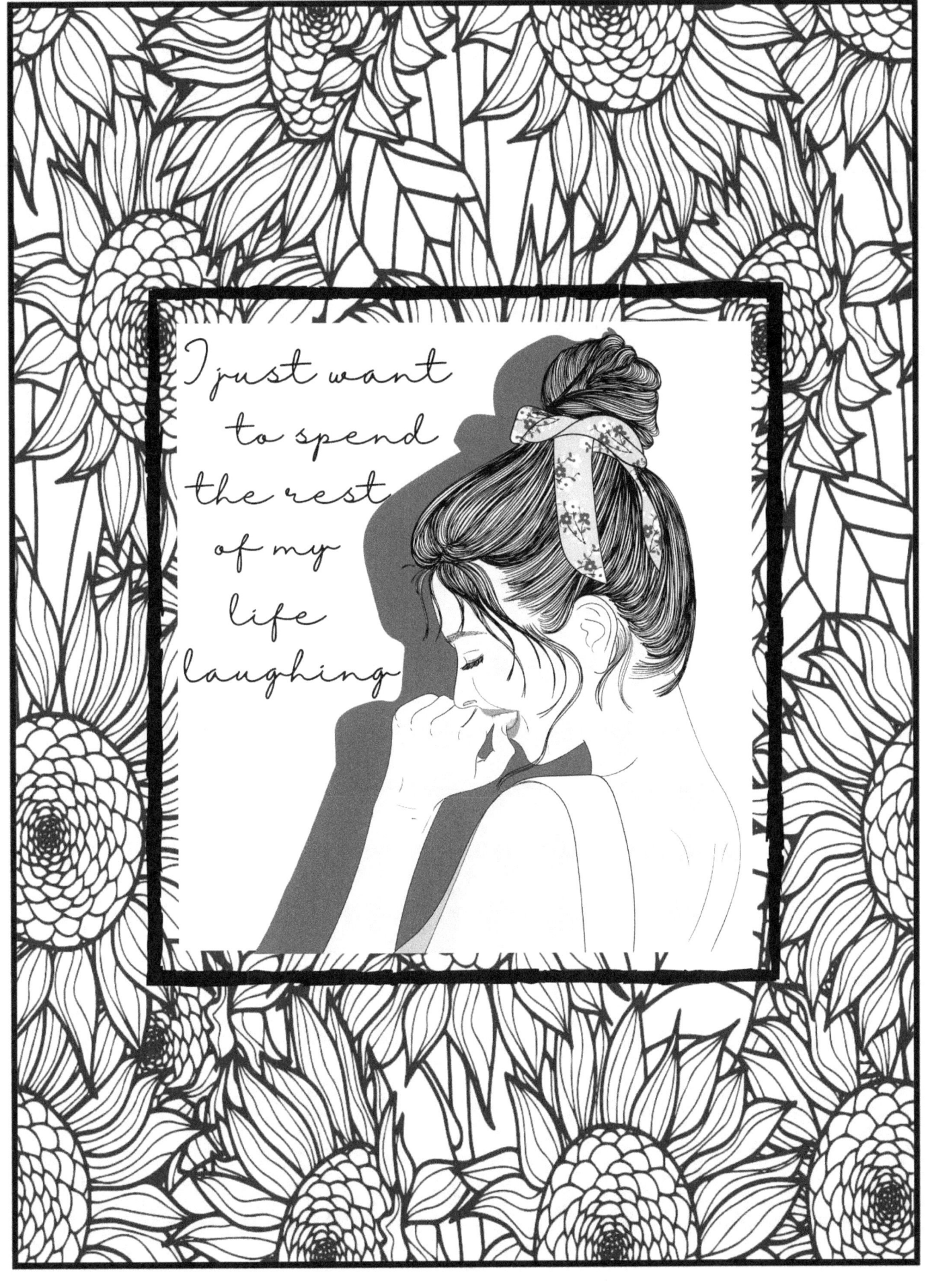

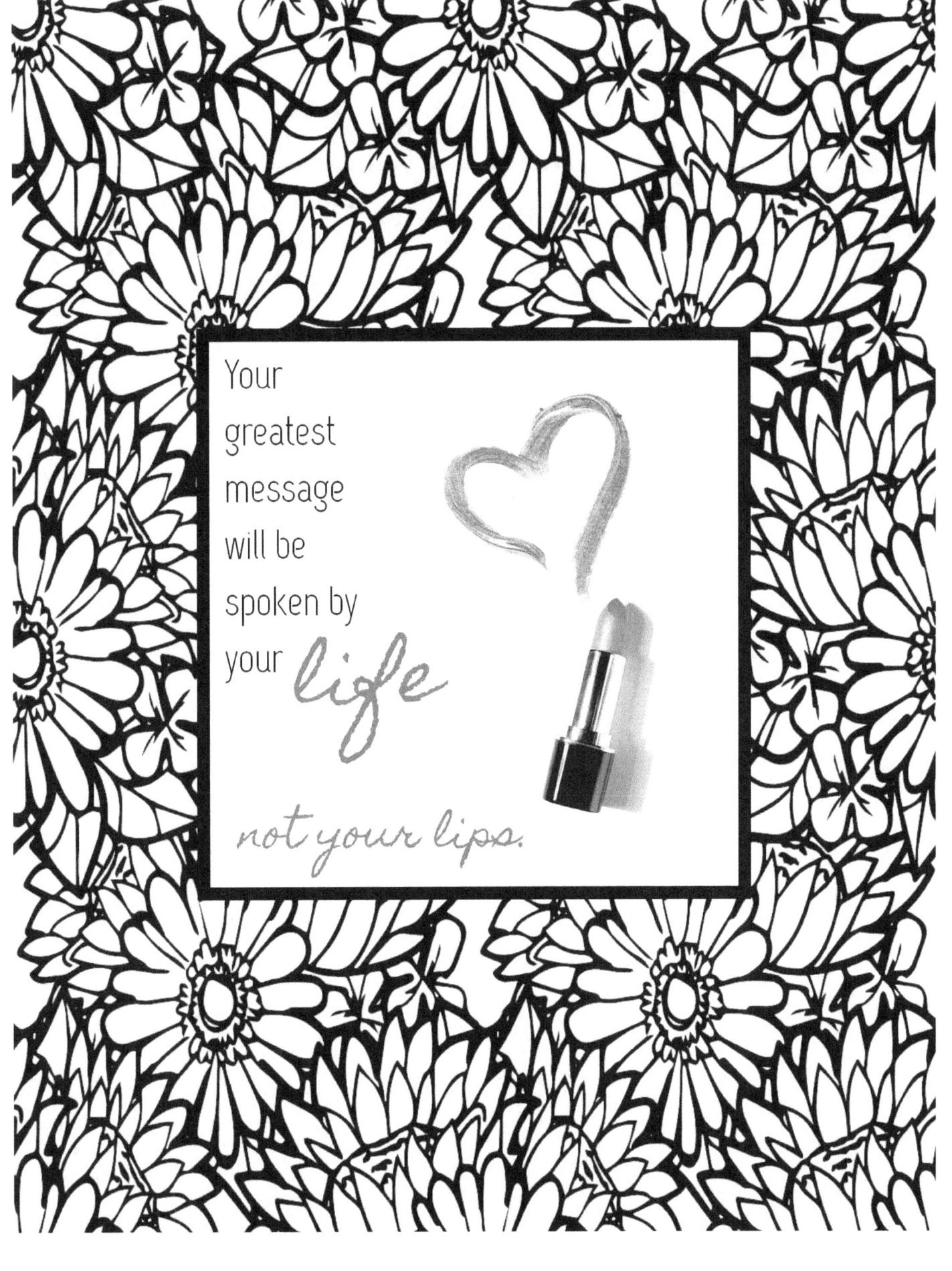

Your greatest message will be spoken by your *life* not your lips.

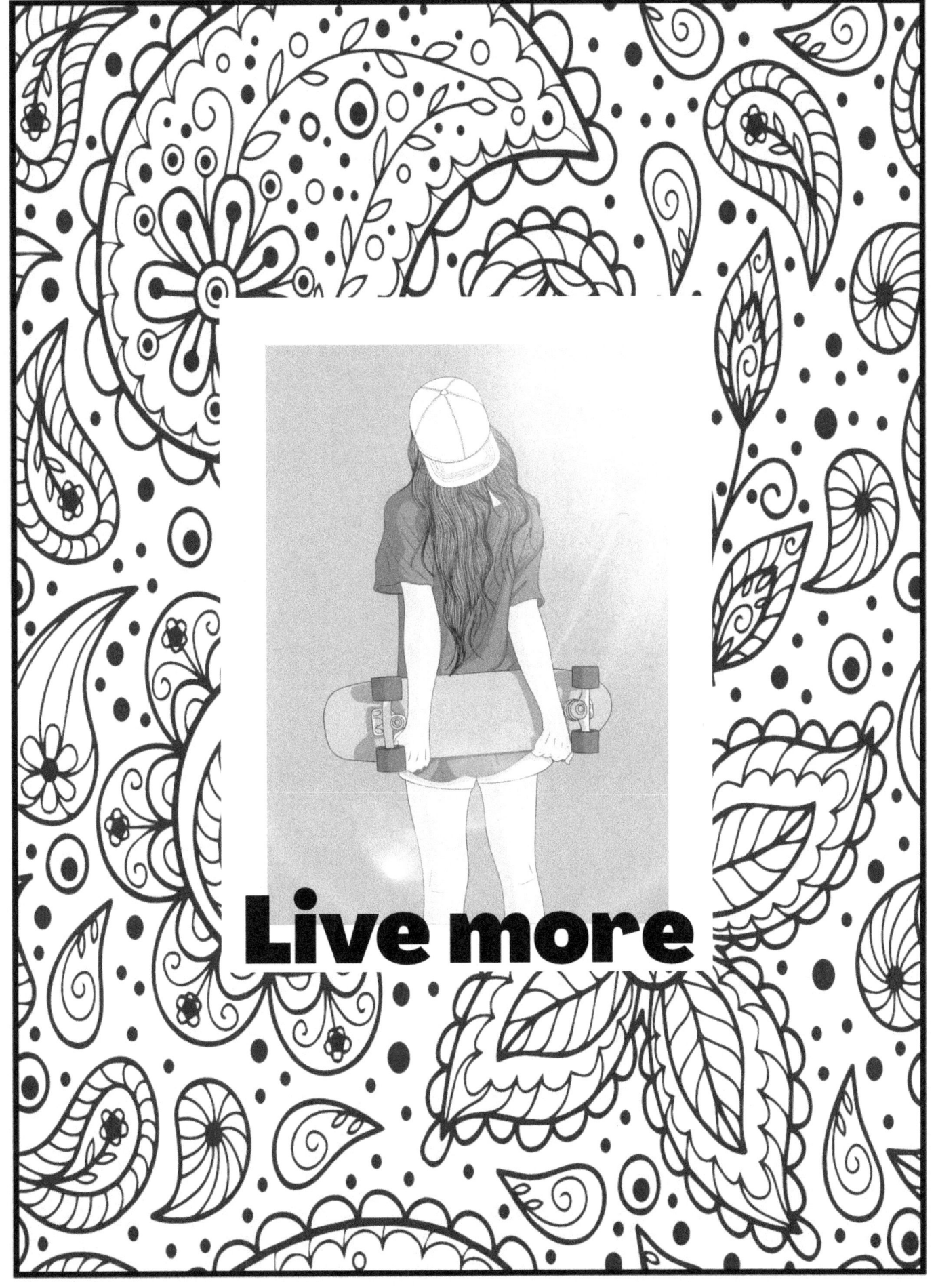

Live more

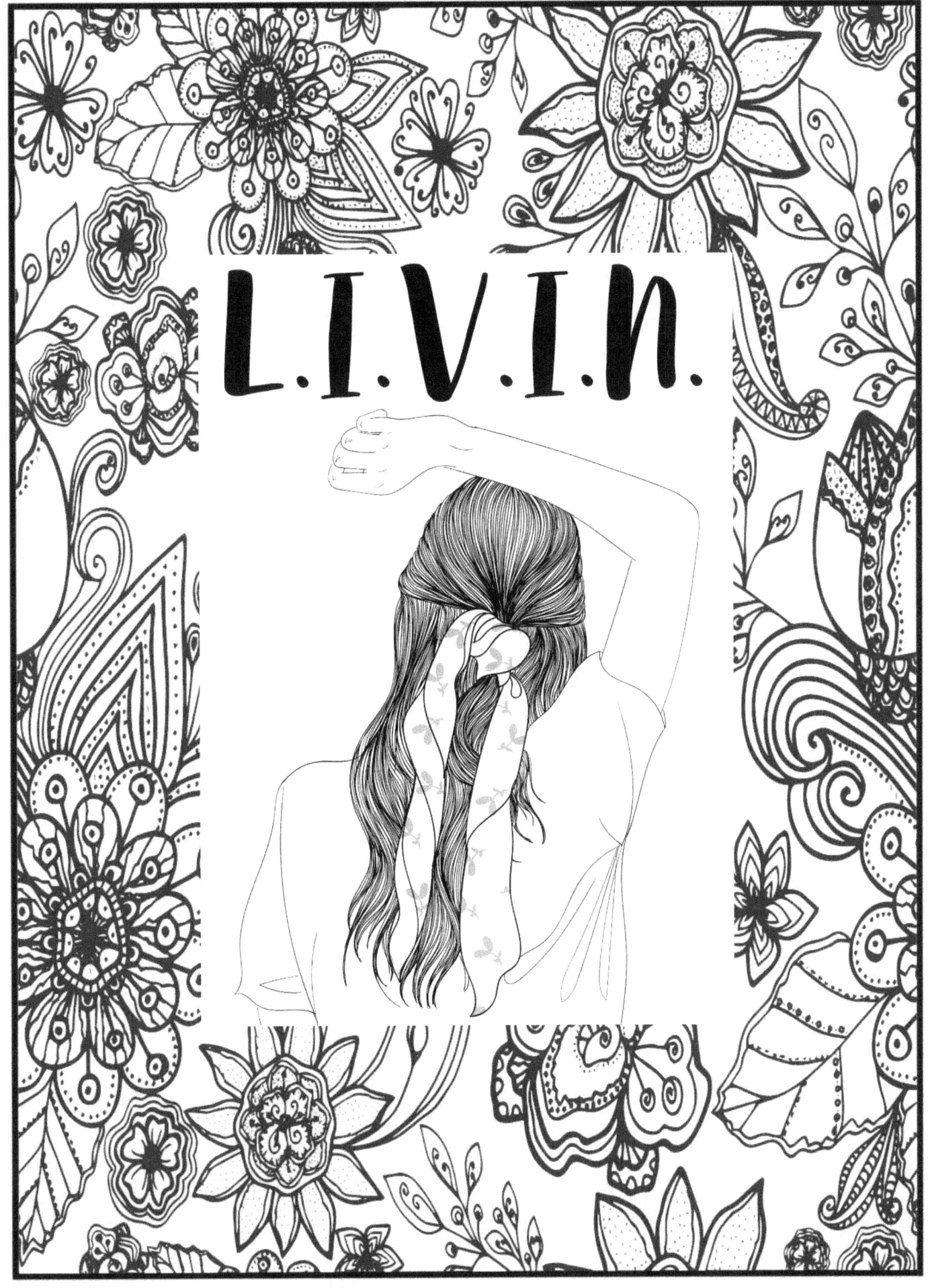

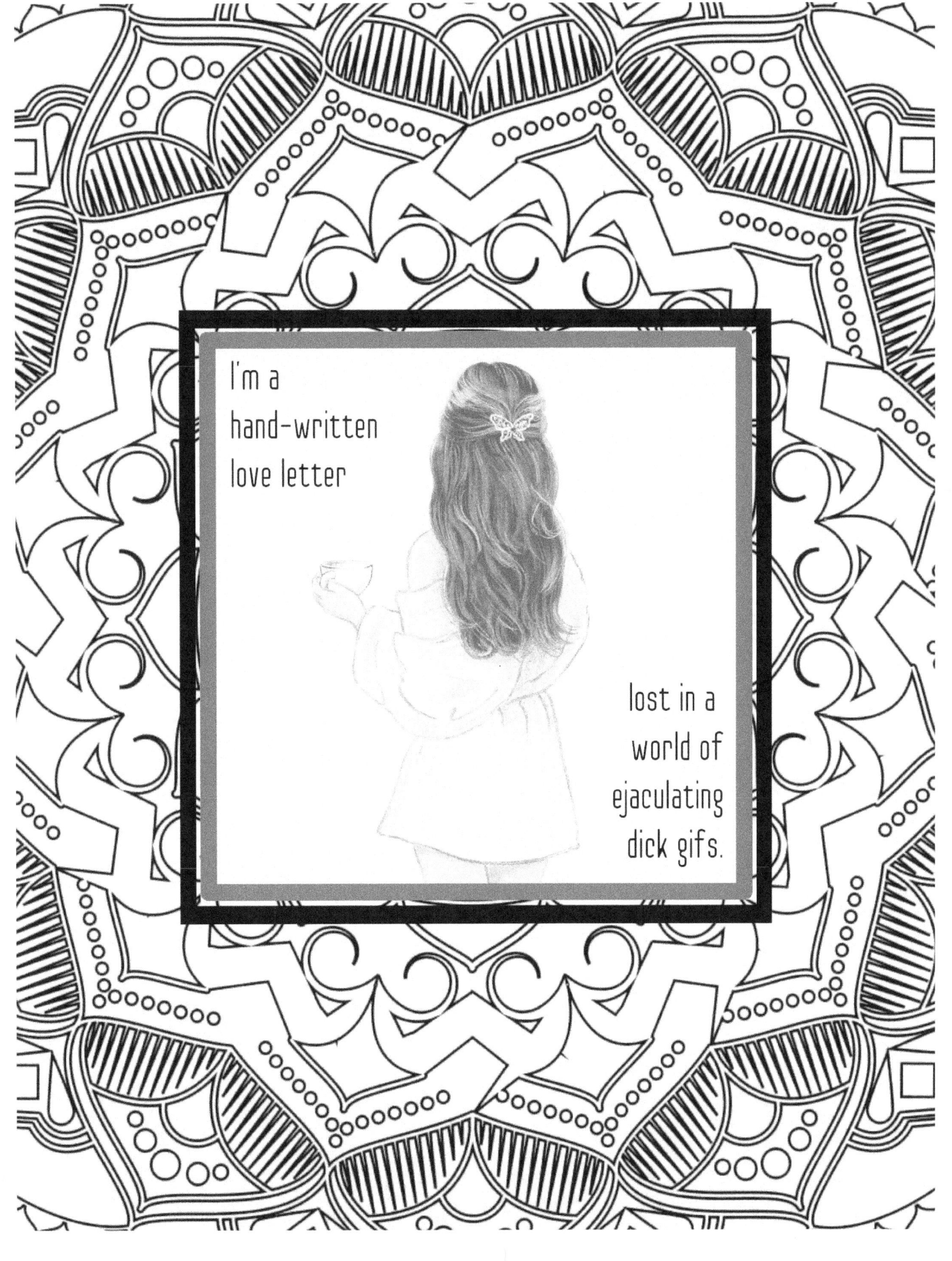

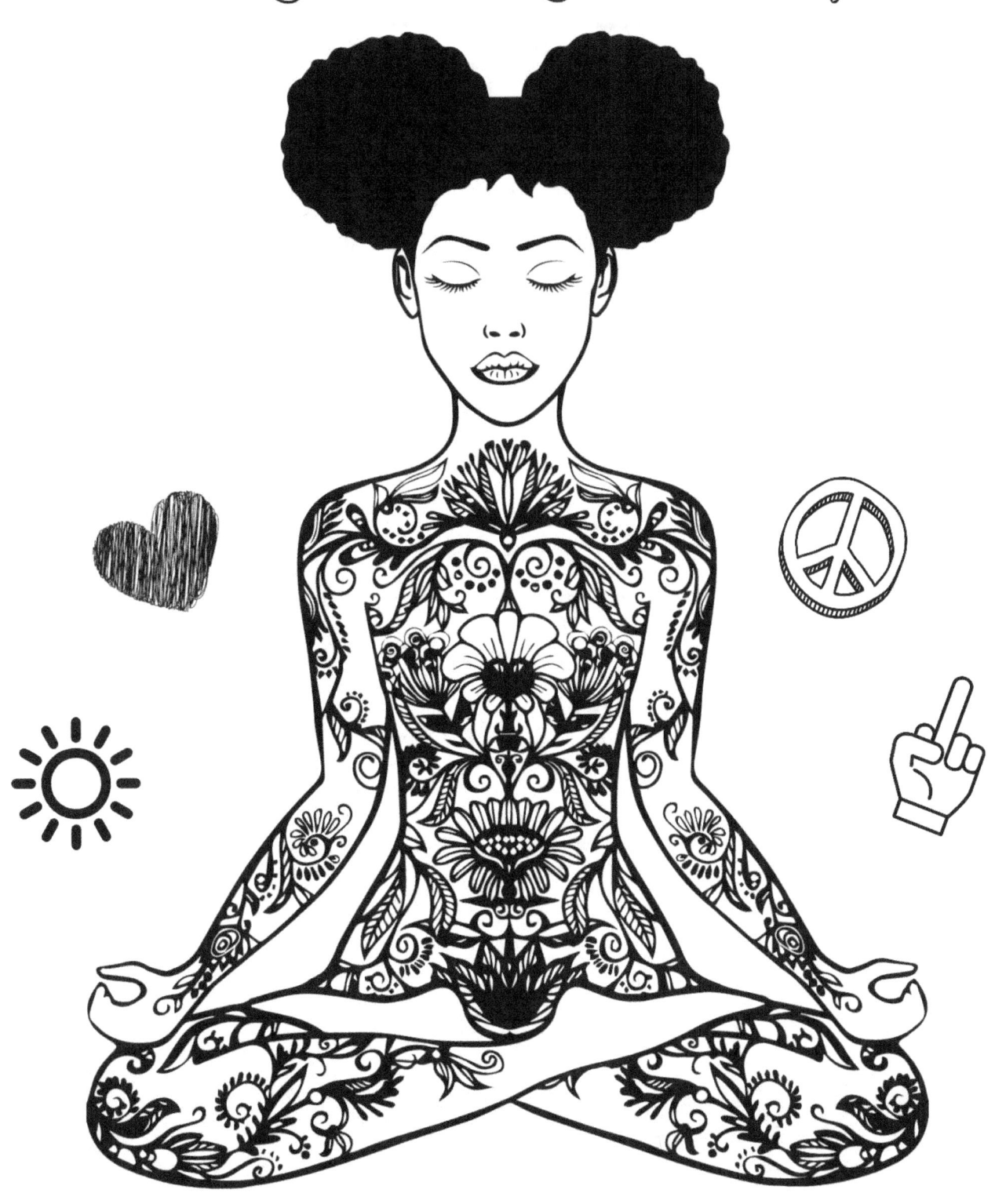

I'm mostly love, light, and peace.

With a little bit of Fuck Off

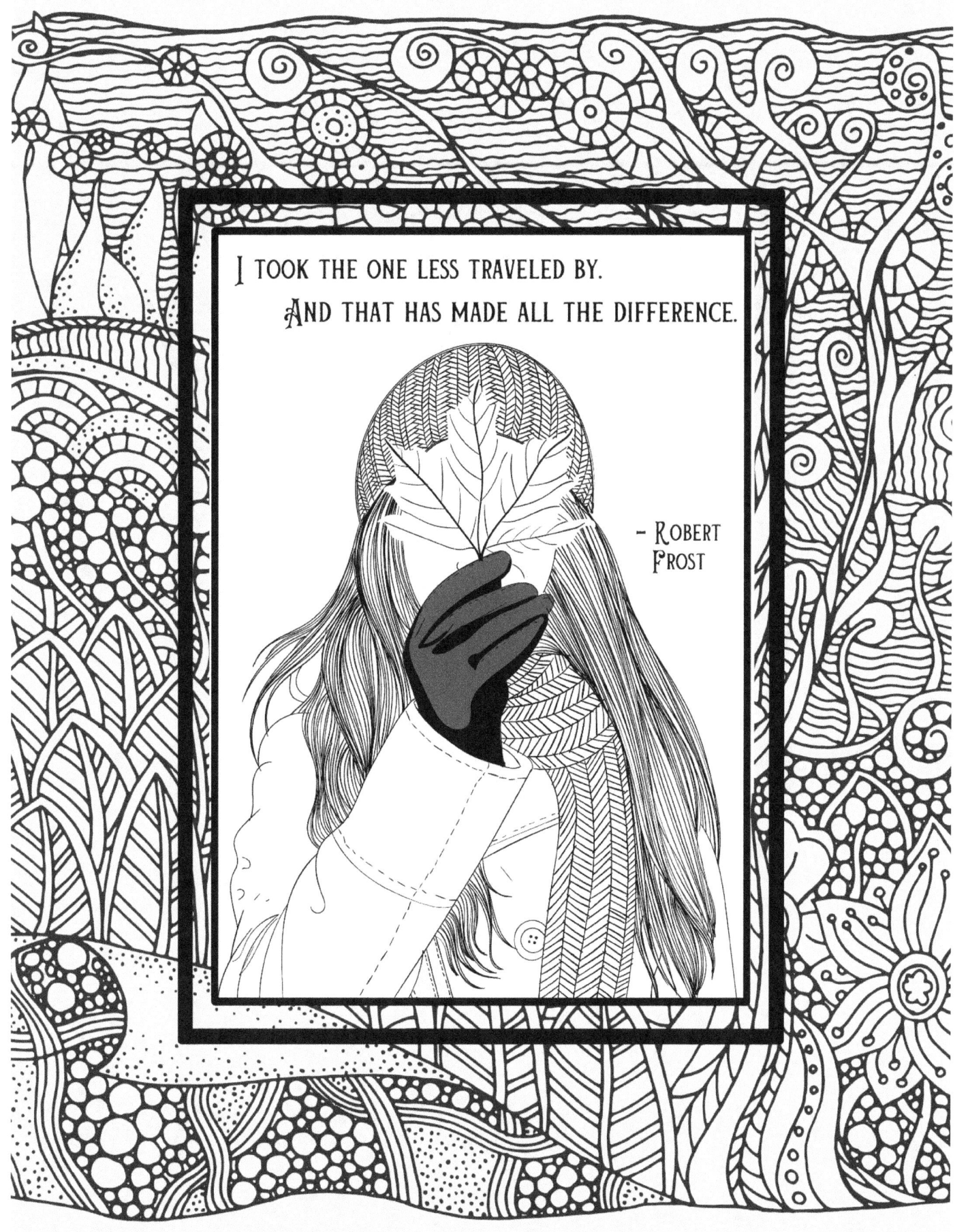

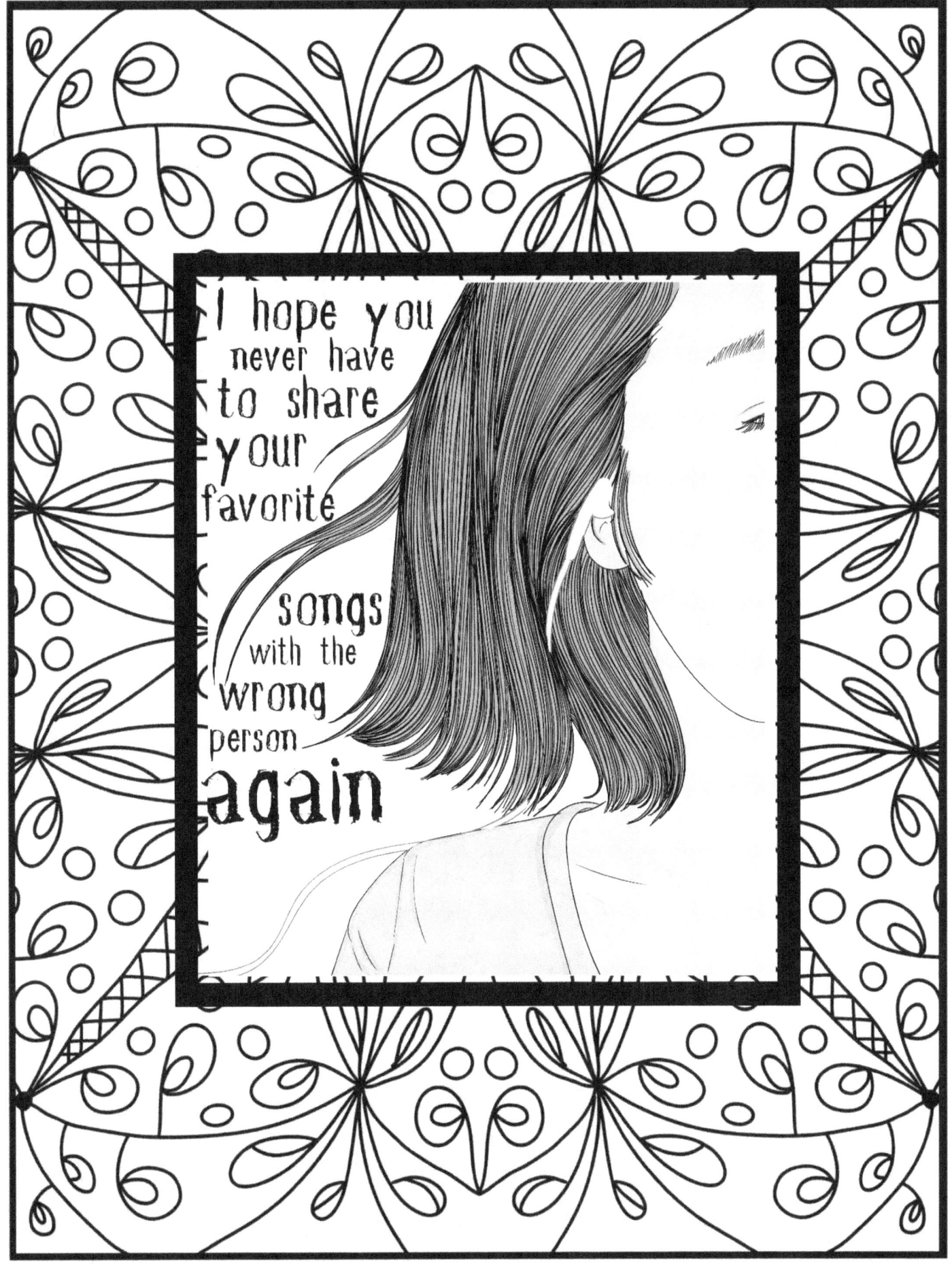

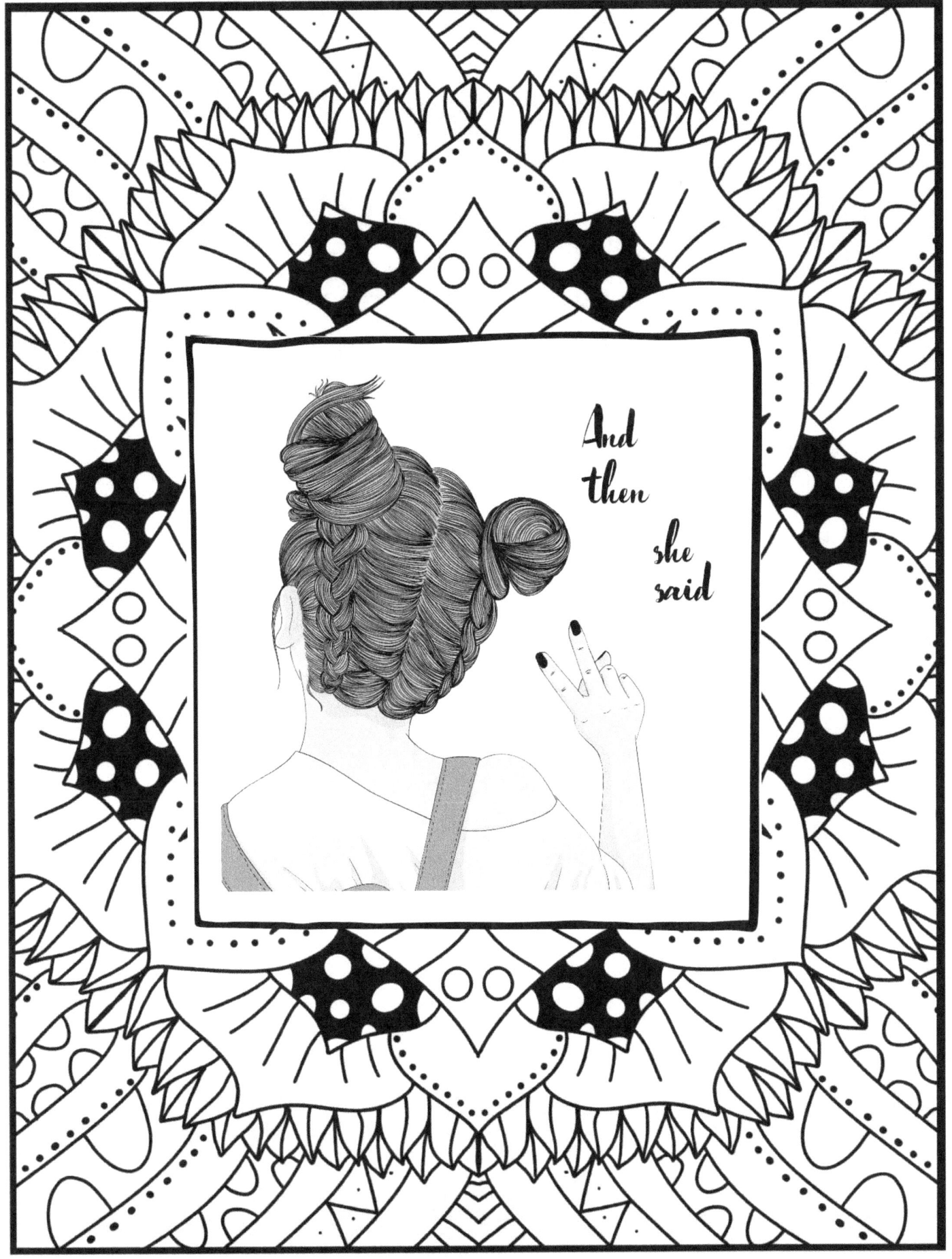

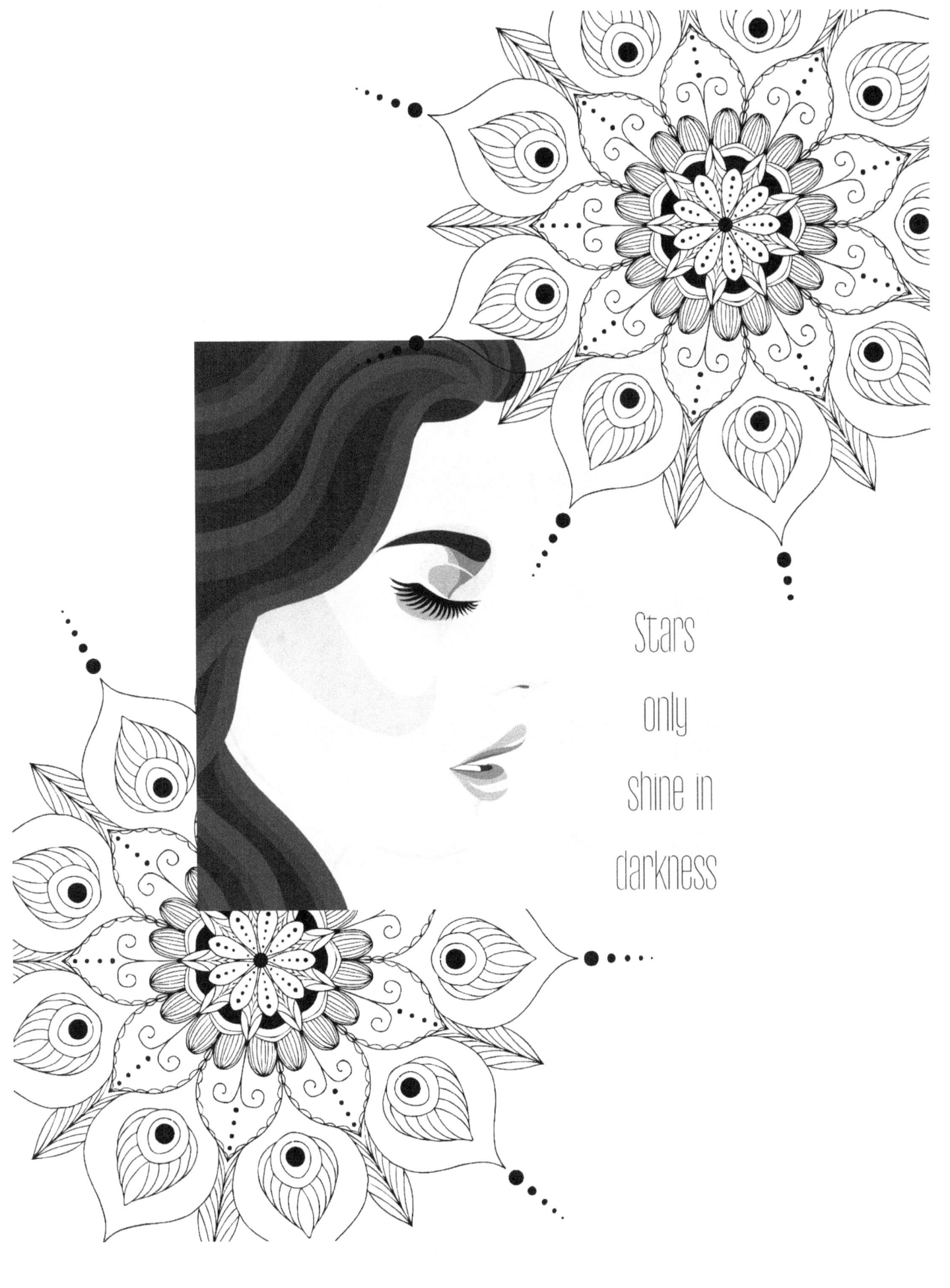

Stars
only
shine in
darkness

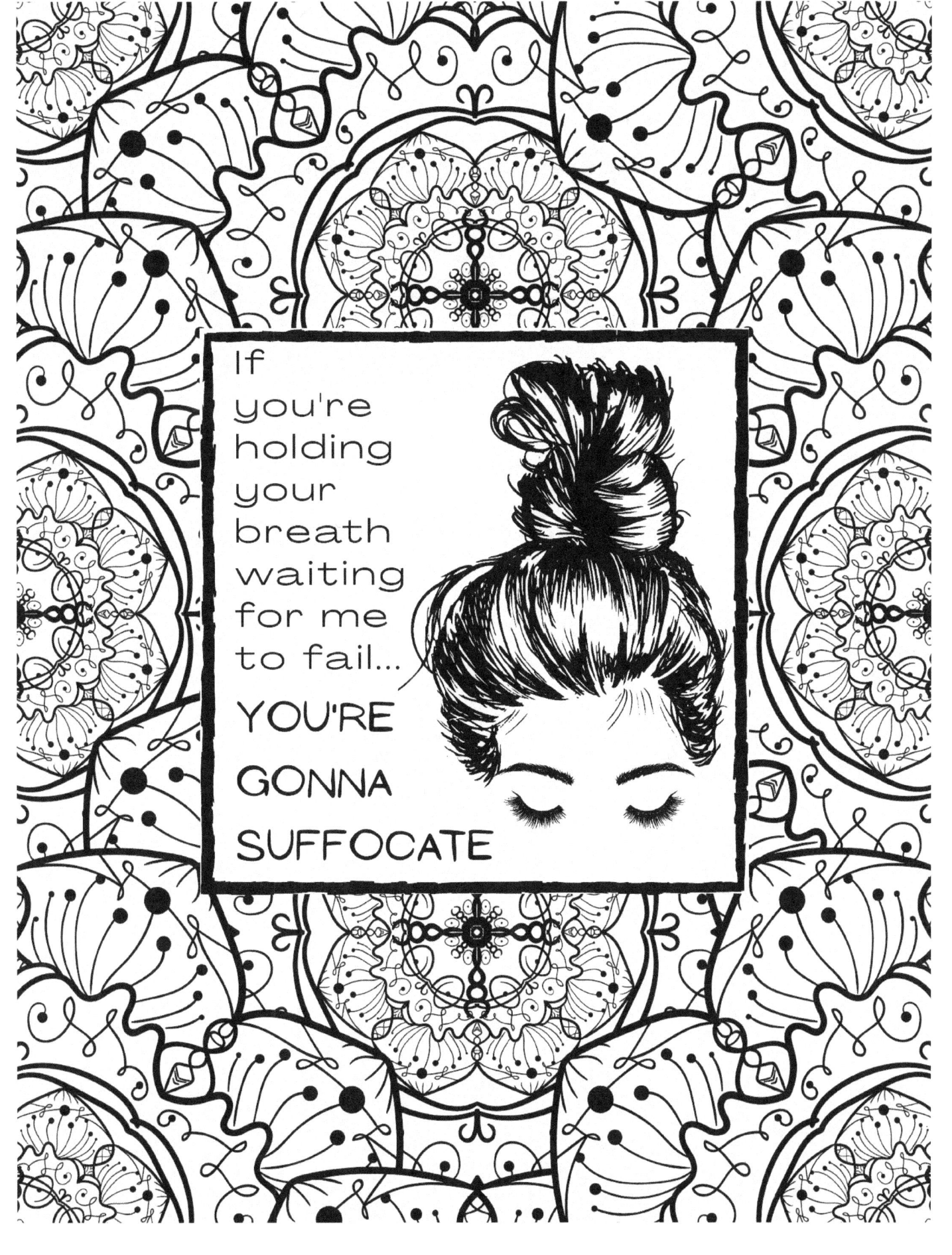

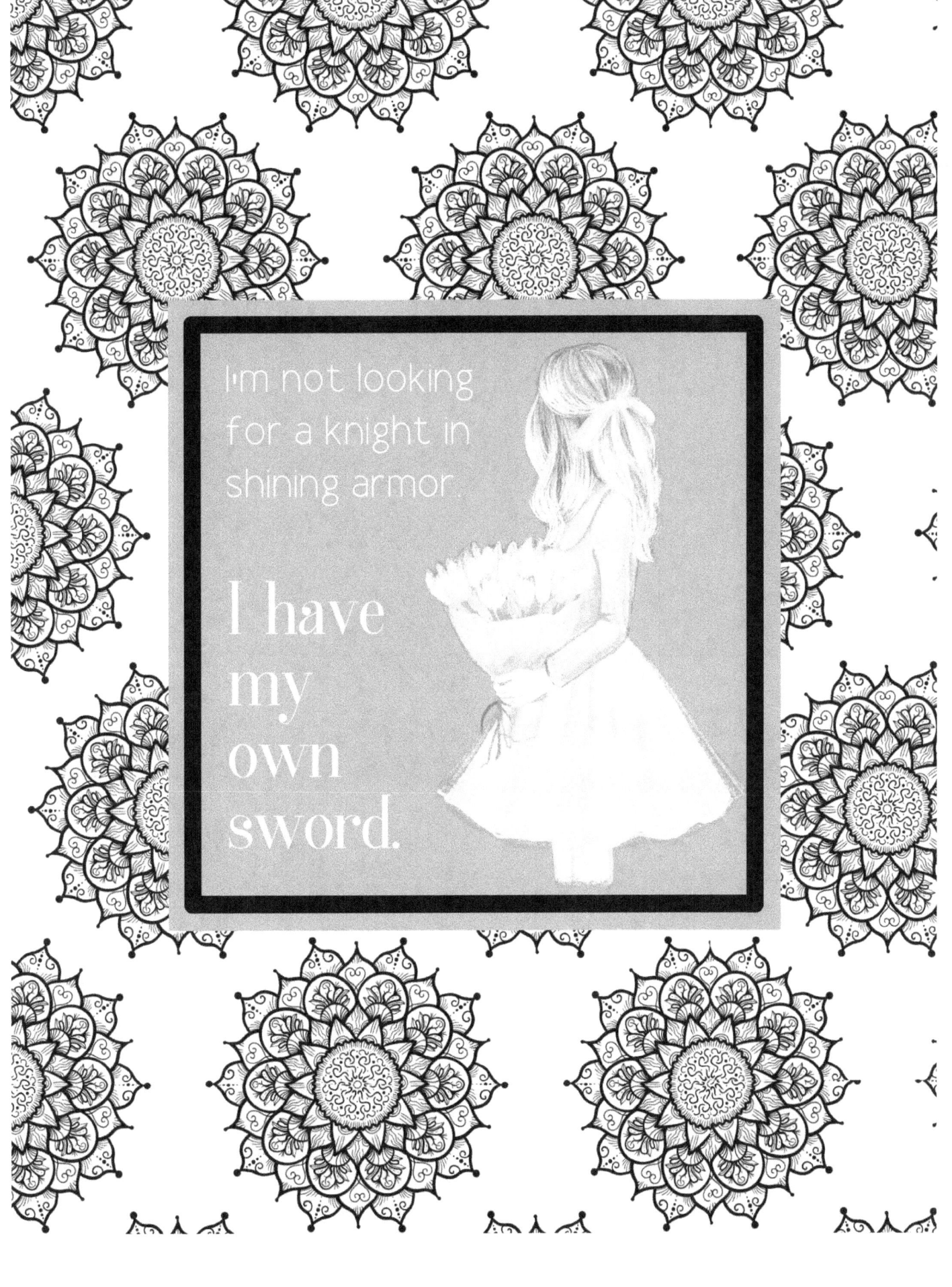

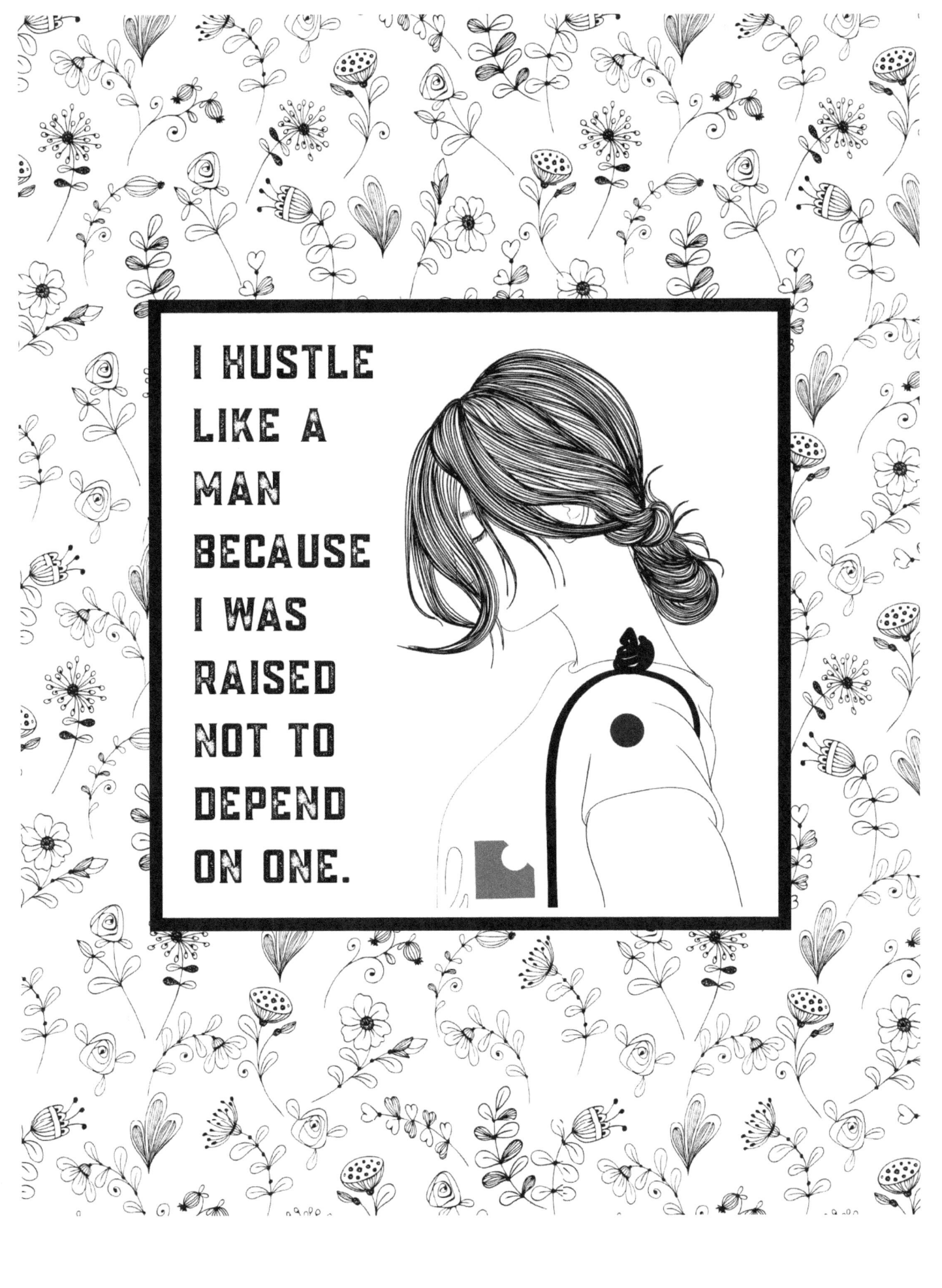

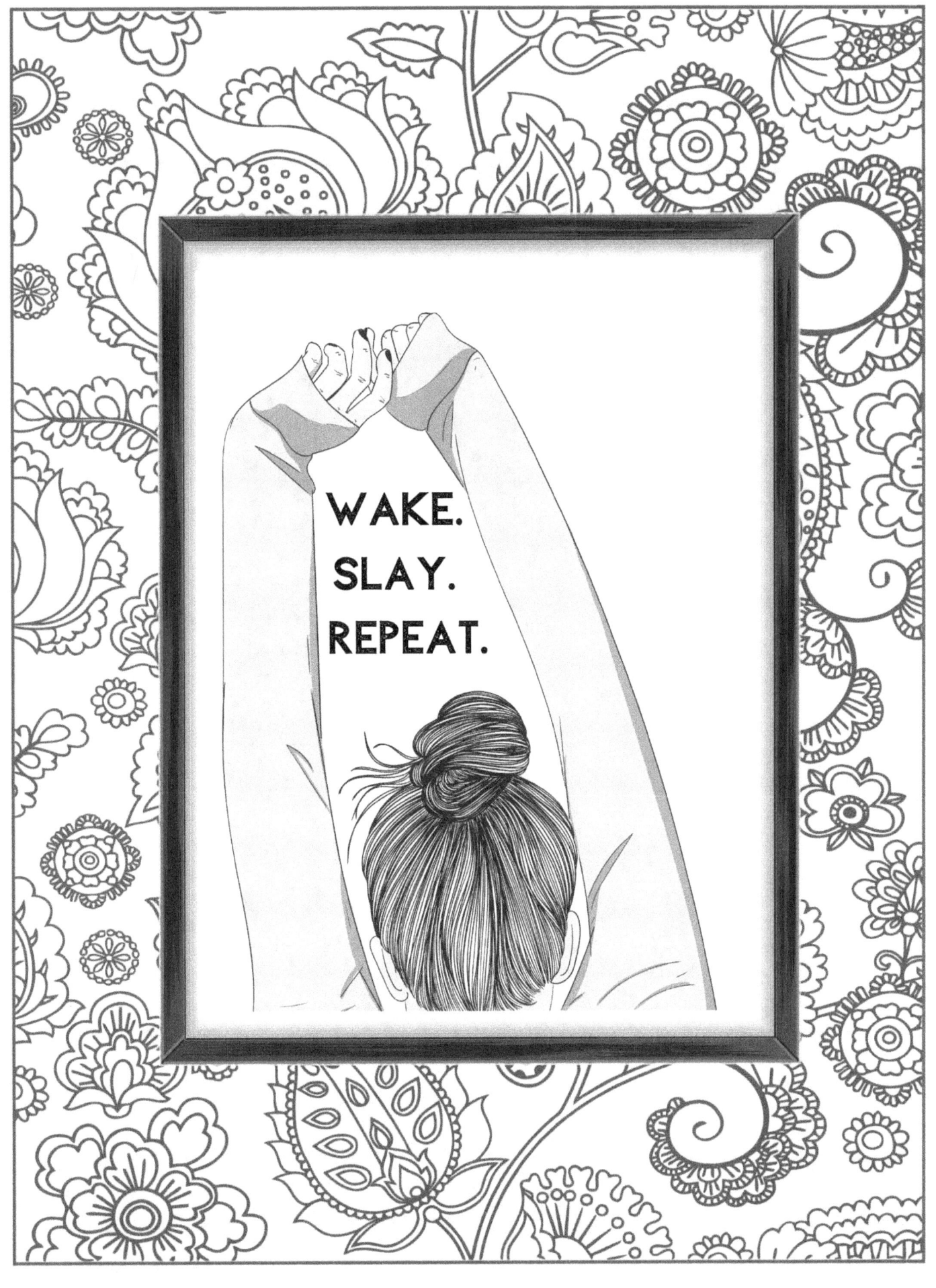

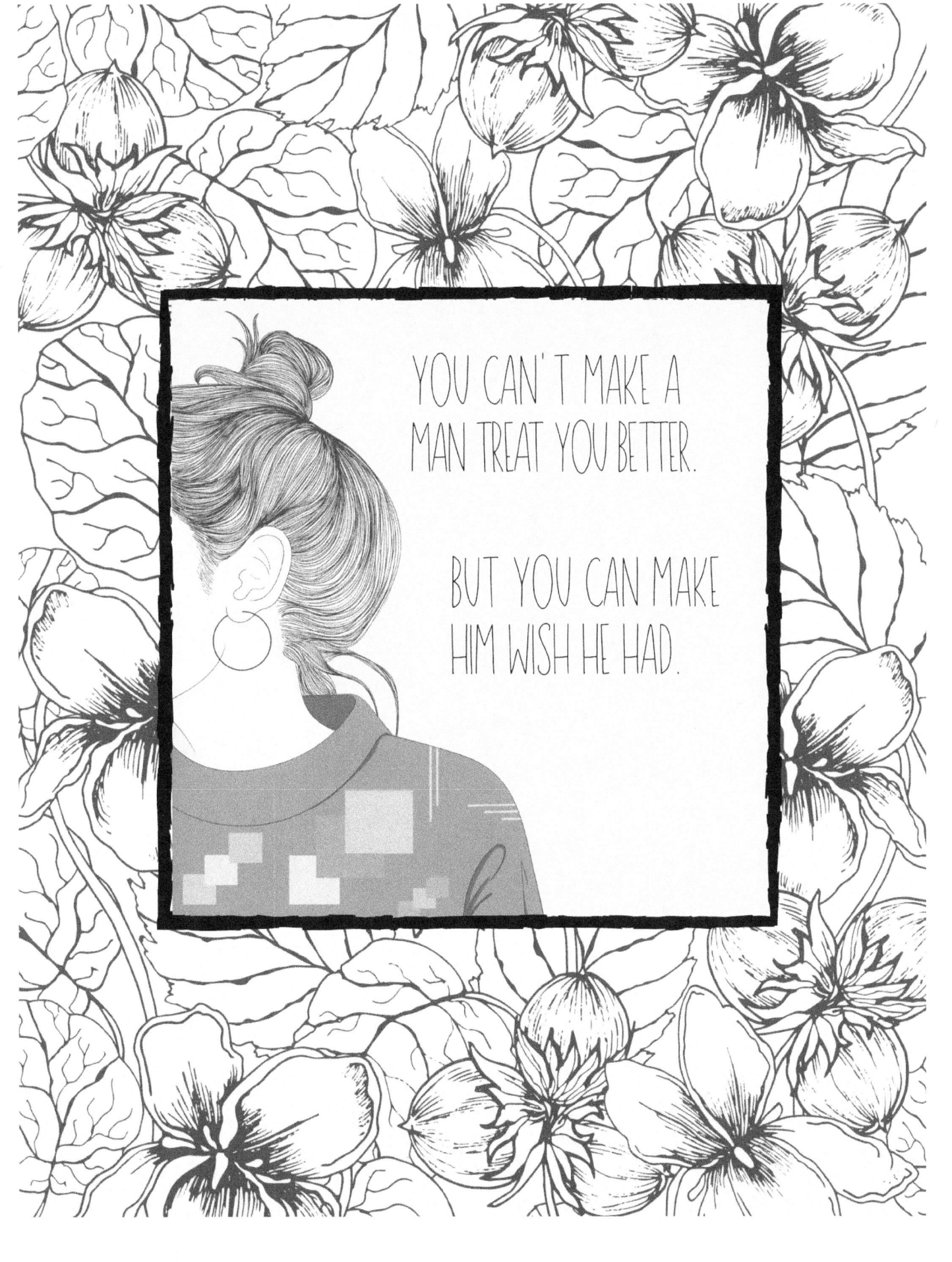

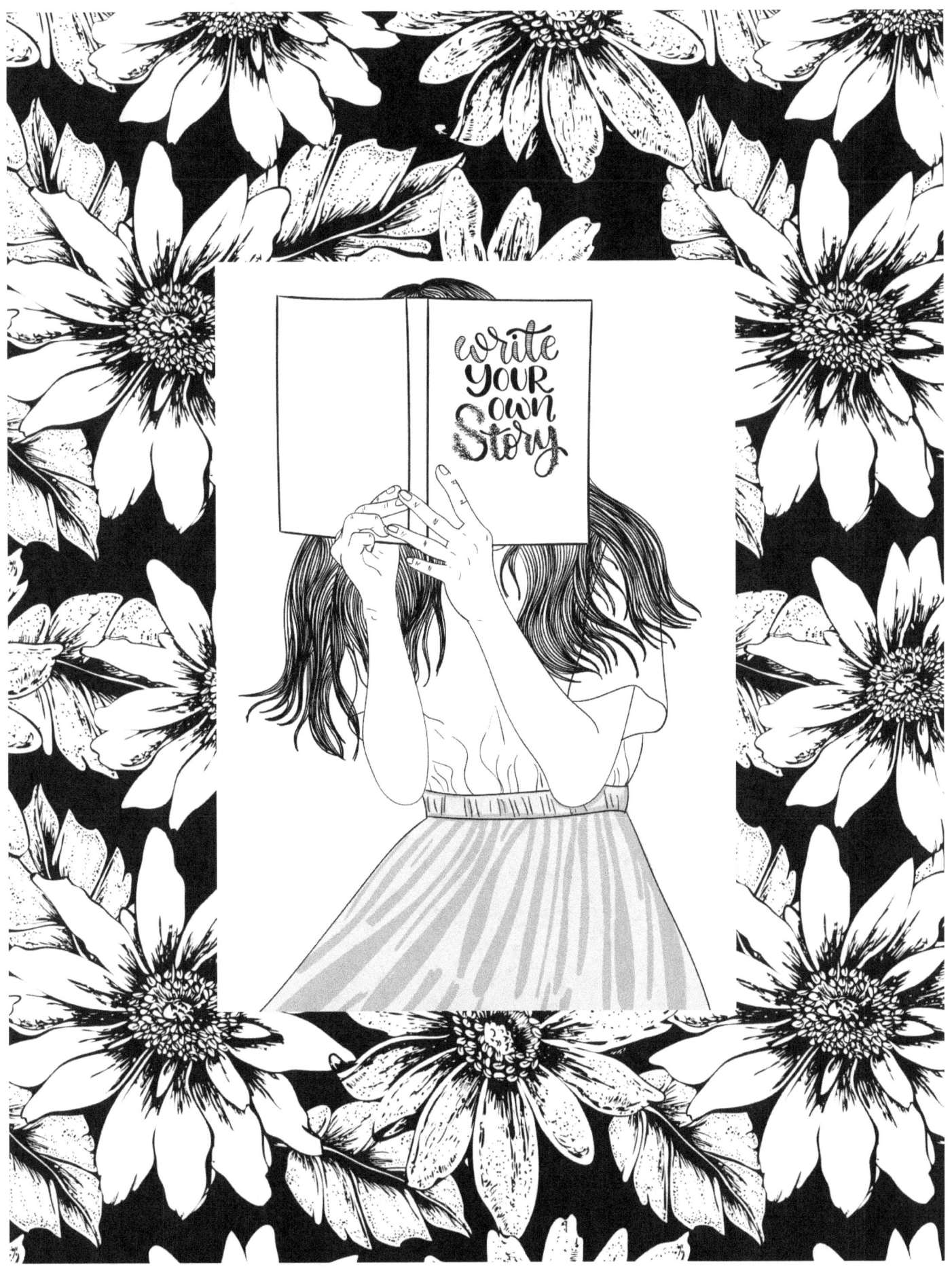

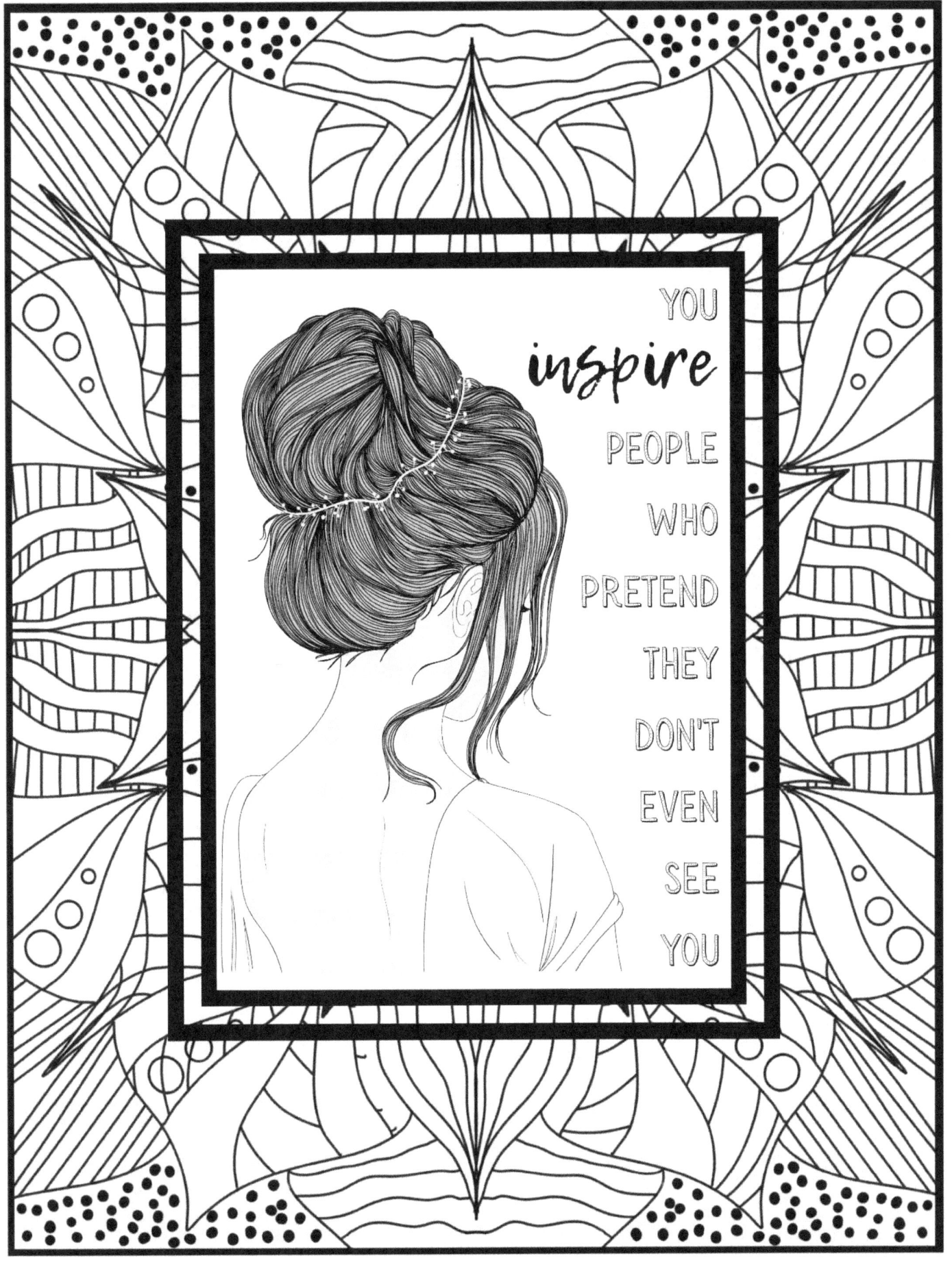